THE
MAKING OF AMERICA
SERIES

SUNLAND
AND TUJUNGA
FROM VILLAGE TO CITY

CASTLE–STYLE HOME. It is possible to see the diversity that is a result of the "rugged individualists" who settled in Tujunga. There have been homes of all styles, even castles. This one was torn down for freeway access c. 1970.

THE
MAKING OF AMERICA
SERIES

SUNLAND AND TUJUNGA

FROM VILLAGE TO CITY

MARLENE A. HITT
LITTLE LANDERS HISTORICAL SOCIETY

ARCADIA

Copyright © 2002 by Marlene A. Hitt
ISBN 0-7385-2377-1

Published by Arcadia Publishing,
Charleston SC, Chicago IL, Portsmouth NH, San Francisco CA

First published 2002
Reprinted 2003

Printed in the United States

Library of Congress control number: 2002102842

For all general information contact Arcadia Publishing at:
Telephone 843-853-2070
Fax 843-853-0044
E-Mail sales@arcadiapublishing.com
For customer service and orders:
Toll-Free 1-888-313-2665

Visit us on the Internet at www.arcadiapublishing.com

CONTENTS

ACKNOWLEDGMENTS

Through the years, many people have seen the value of preserving the history of the area that was Rancho Tujunga. The photographer Harry Lamson left a pictorial history. The *Record Ledger* newspaper provided over 60 years worth of stories and news events. Oral histories have been recorded, documents unearthed, maps preserved, books written, artifacts collected, and stories told. This material is preserved in Bolton Hall Museum in Tujunga, California.

A small group of dedicated neighbors once had to fight to save Bolton Hall, built in 1913 as the centerpiece of the Little Lands Colony. The hall had become derelict by 1959 when the city of Los Angeles voted to tear it down. Under the leadership of one dedicated woman, Roberta Stewart, the building was saved. Bolton Hall was reopened in 1980 and made the home of the Little Landers Historical Society.

The collections were preserved, added to, and made available for the citizens of Sunland, Tujunga, and surrounding areas. Today, the museum is the hub of historical information for children and adults alike, a place for visitors from all over the world, and a "clubhouse" for the historical society and citizens of the area.

The members of the Little Landers Historical Society of Bolton Hall Museum have for many years been collecting, organizing, and preserving the history of the place once known as the Rancho Tujunga. It is to all the members of the Little Landers Historical Society that this work is dedicated.

Though every attempt has been made to be accurate, it must be said that this is a popular history, rather than a historical document. The attempt is to show the soul of a people and a place. I am grateful for the opportunity to show the rich history and colorful folklore of the area, an isolated suburb of Los Angeles in southern California. The whole of the story stands as tribute to all people who have, at one time or another, entered a new frontier.

Photographs and images shown here are courtesy of Ray Brunke, with his collection of Lamson, Ansel Kickbush, Kamshroer, Elliott, and John Robinson photographs, along with the *Record Ledger* collection and assorted other photograph donations.

I am especially grateful to Martha Houk, director of Bolton Hall Museum and consultant for this project; Genevieve Krueger, who was gracious enough to read the manuscript; and Lloyd Hitt, for photographs.

INTRODUCTION

There has always been something special about the foothill communities of southern California. The climate is mild. A breeze blows through the canyons every afternoon to clear the air. The mountains rise above the valley floor, seeming majestic, surrounding and surpassing human frailty and faults. To watch the changing colors on these folds and peaks at the end of the day is something to look forward to. The afternoon shadows on the yuccas and chaparral in the Big Tujunga Wash inspire artists and poets.

The settlers came with something like "pure cussedness," eccentricity, and "rugged individualism," attributes that continue to this day. The people are determined to be adequately recognized by the city of Los Angeles. The area once known as the Rancho Tujunga is on the edge of the city and had always been easy to ignore. Part of the appeal, then, is this stubborn determination of real down-to-earth folks who stick together. And they must, since there have been and will be hard times.

The most enticing and lovable aspect of Sunland-Tujunga is its history. Like many such settlements, it began small and grew into part of a metropolis. The people who settled on the land showed strength, persistence, and ingenuity, and acted often in the spirit of fun. Not always, but most of the time. The history of this area is the history of the settling of the west. The land itself often made the choices as to the direction the pioneers took.

From the 1880s to the present, the population has grown from a few adventurers to hundreds of thousands of people. The group that was once a raggedy bunch of rugged individualists is now a part of the great city of Los Angeles. Once an agricultural area, Sunland (Monte Vista) was a quiet and very beautiful village.

The Little Landers Colony, formed higher up in the valley in Tujunga, was in the beginning a socialist utopian colony that quickly grew into a business, social, and cultural community: the city of Tujunga.

Through the years, keeping in mind the full meaning of rugged individualism, the community has struggled through the building of a civilized society, the Great Depression, the war years, the coming of bikers and hippies, the drug culture, busing, suburbanites, and the rise and fall of the economy. Even during decline, followed by persistent attempts at renewal, success, failure, and more renewal, the citizens have worked together.

The turn of the century finds a whole new group of pioneers, as families from other countries forge new businesses and establish homes and lives. Over the years, this place has been called "the beautiful vale of Monte Vista," "the healthiest place in the world," "the Rock," and "the Armpit of the City." All could be true, depending on the observer. Whatever the truth, families stay here for generations. Many residents stay because of the solitude on the edge of the metropolis of Los Angeles where there are miles and miles of rugged wilderness areas, yet it is close enough to drive to work. The place takes hold and people love it, no matter what.

WORKING MEN. These are the workers—men who cleared the fields, built the buildings, and put out the fires. Every man was expected to carry a shovel, especially in summer, in case fire broke out.

1. THE LAND WAS WAITING

It was to an already occupied land that the Lopez cattle ranchers came to the towns we now know as Sunland, Tujunga, Lake View Terrace, and Shadow Hills. People had been living there for many centuries. The Tujunga Native Americans had occupied the land for at least 3,000 years before the Shoshone came into the area. An estimate made in 1980 suggested that 260,000 people of an Uto-Aztecan Shoshonean language group had at one time migrated from the Great Basin area into what is now southern California.

The towns of Monte Vista (later named Sunland) and the Little Lands Colony (later becoming the city of Tujunga) developed in what is considered by geographers to lie in a rift between the San Gabriel and the Verdugo Mountains. Lying at the base of the San Gabriel Mountains, part of the transverse ranges of Southern California, the communities are situated below the foothills for about 6 miles with an approximate area of 12 square miles. The elevation of Sunland is about 1,200 feet, while the slopes of Tujunga rise to about 2,200 feet.

Intersecting the San Gabriel Mountains is the Big Tujunga River, once a year-round waterway and depended upon as the major source of water by all the people that have lived on this dry terrain. On the floor of the valley, settlers found several kinds of game, as well as the many other materials used by Native Americans and earlier settlers. The river and wash bed covers a wide swath of land made up of sand, gravel, and unique plants that are an important part of the natural environment. The foothills and mountains contained an abundance of materials.

The Big Tujunga Canyon, cutting through the west end of the valley, carries large volumes of water from the mountain watershed during the rainy seasons, depositing soil and rocks of decomposed granite as the flood waters rush through it. This pattern creates deep alluvium and acres of silt which, over the centuries, has built up into rich deposits of soil. At one time, the name Tujunga was thought to have meant "Big Thunder" because of the sound of boulders being washed down the canyon. The water from the Big Tujunga watershed empties south into the Los Angeles River. The ancient trails over the mountains lead northeast to the Mojave Desert.

The land once known as Rancho Tujunga lay between two missions, the Mission San Fernando Rey de España and Mission San Gabriel Archangel. When the Spanish came, along with the chain of missions, they named the native people according to the name of the mission established. Thus, the native group living closest to the Mission San Gabriel became "Gabrielinos," while those living near the Mission San Fernando were called "Fernandenos." The padres called the people in the Rancho Tujunga area "Gabrielinos."

John Peabody Harrington of the Smithsonian Institute, who was described by Carl S. Denzel, director of the Southwest Museum in Los Angeles, as the most distinguished anthropologist to have studied the Native Americans of California, interviewed Gabrielinos in the early 1900s. He found that the name Tujunga meant "old woman's place" (the old woman in this case meaning "our grandmother the earth"). In the Gabrielino dialect, the ending "nga" means "the place of" and "Tuhu" means "the old woman."

In southern California, the oldest habitation of native people was said to be in the village of Tujunga, occupied since *c.* 435 by as many as 1,000 residents. These native people had a highly developed civilization. In 1945 and again in 1965, archaeological studies were made that indicated that the early people had a structured way of life, active trading with other groups, and a complex language. The baskets they made are considered some of the finest produced. At one site near the mouth of the Big Tujunga River, there was an elaborate place created for the mourning ritual of the many groups in the greater area. Our present information tells us that these people called themselves the Tongva.

BIG TUJUNGA RIVER. This canyon river and the land around it provided sustenance for all living creatures.

It is written that these Native Americans were of a carefree, happy disposition, loving music and dancing. Their instruments were rattles and flutes. These Hunter-gatherer people used the natural environment. Food came from yucca root, acorns, small game, fish, and various plant sources. Clothing was sparse and typically made from plants and animals. Wickiups, the native dwellings, were built of willow and grasses. Life was peaceful and rich and the people were brave and resourceful.

William McCawley, author of *The First Angelinos*, recorded his own account:

> Although the basic lifestyle of the Gabrielinos was that of hunter-gatherers, the wealth of food and natural resources in the Gabrielino homeland, coupled with their strategic location between the Chumash Indians to the northwest and the other Uto-Aztecan Indians to the south and east, allowed them to build a complex society of significant economic power and cultural influence. The Gabrielino homeland became a cultural melting pot in which the Uto-Aztecan tradition met and fused with the vigorous maritime-oriented culture of the coastal Chumash to create a society of immense vitality and creativity. As a result, the Gabrielino are regarded as having been one of the most materially rich and culturally influential Indian groups of southern California.

The first European explorers left their mark on the land with Cabrillo's visit in 1542 and Sir Frances Drake's expedition in 1579. The actual settlement by the Spanish did not occur, however, until 1769 and extended to 1822.

The Franciscan Padres, particularly Junipero Serra, were instrumental in founding a string of missions along the coast of California. Serra was a Spanish missionary who was given the tremendous job by King Charles III of building mission settlements along the coast of upper California. Father Serra was 56 years old at the time and had done remarkably well with the Native Americans in Baja, California. The king wanted to extend the mission chain and chose Serra for the job. He established nine missions from San Diego to Monterey, and had made arrangements for building more.

From the soil around them, the padres built churches and mission compounds in a new and raw country. The remote colonial province of California was once part of the mighty Spanish Empire. With a military escort, the padres opened the missions of San Fernando and San Gabriel. San Gabriel, founded in 1771, was a wayside stop beside three well-traveled trails on a crossroads passing north to south and east to west. This mission was constantly overrun by the military. The soldiers' poor behavior was a constant trial to the mission fathers and contributed to the mission's constant trouble with the Native Americans.

Mission San Gabriel was prosperous in its own right and was also considered to be the spiritual and cultural center of the vast ranches. In time, the mission at San Gabriel grew so prosperous that it was named "Queen of the Missions." It

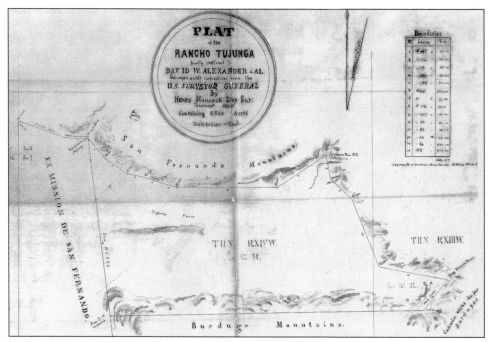

RANCHO TUJUNGA PLAT MAP. This original plat map for the Rancho Tujunga, dated 1840, shows boundaries marked as "Gray Granite Rock," "Sycamore Tree," and "Live Oak."

was situated in a valley offering fine timber and pasturage, as well as plenty of water for irrigation. San Gabriel Mission became famous for its fine wines. Soap-making, tallow-rendering, weaving, and leather work were important industries.

At the Mission San Fernando, founded in 1797, the padres found that, in addition to congenial Native Americans, the valley around San Fernando showed potential for agricultural development. The presence of four springs, flowing as though they would never run dry, strongly influenced the padres' decision to settle there. A small chapel was erected, then a granary, a storeroom, and a weaving room. A growing congregation made it necessary in only a year to build a larger church. Within seven years, there were nearly 1,000 converts. Cattle raising was the dominant industry. In 1819, there were 21,000 head of livestock, primarily for the flourishing trade in tallow and hides, as well as the crafting of leather. The mission also produced a bounty of olives, fruits, nuts, grapes, and field crops.

By 1822, Spanish rule had yielded to the Mexican government and the secularization of the missions by the Mexicans began. Between 1833 and 1842, the mission lands were converted into more than 300 ranchos granted to Mexican citizens. Local historian Viola Carlson wrote: "Altogether almost 800 land grants were made during the Mexican regime which ended in 1848 with the treaty of Guadalupe Hidalgo and, two years later, California became a part of the United States."

The communities which are now Sunland, Tujunga, Lake View Terrace, and Shadow Hills are roughly situated on a parcel of land consisting of 6,660.71 acres (1.5 square Mexican leagues). Originally, the plot was granted to Francisco and Pedro Lopez by the Mexican government in 1840 and was called the Rancho Tujunga, or *Arroyo de Tujunga*.

Francisco and Pedro Lopez, both born at the San Gabriel Mission, were of Spanish ancestry. Their grandfather, Claudio, was mayordomo of San Gabriel Mission and was later alcalde at the Pueblo de Los Angeles. According to Viola Carlson, author of *Rancho Tujunga, A Mexican Land Grant of 1840*, Francisco was a well-educated man—a gentleman of the period. His brother Pedro worked as mayordomo at the Mission San Fernando Rey de España after the Mexican government took possession in 1834. The Lopez family had become large and influential and had acquired a number of ranchos and adobes in the area. The Tujunga ranch land was needed for the grazing of cattle, horses, and sheep.

Francisco Lopez, while out looking for cattle, discovered gold dust on the roots of wild onions growing near an oak tree in Placerita Canyon, several miles to the north of Rancho Tujunga. Though gold was found in small quantities during mission days, the Lopez discovery was considered the first gold discovery in California, that being in 1842. The first coin put into circulation was from that gold.

The discovery brought prospectors, miners, adventurers, wood choppers, cowboys, outlaws, map-makers, and government surveyors. Those were the first

FRANCISCO LOPEZ. He and his brother Pedro were granted land by the Mexican government in 1840. They called their ranch the Rancho Tujunga.

13

"white men" to venture into this rough and hostile land, where drought and flood vied for prominence, and the fractured and tumbled recent upthrust of mountain terrain was some of the most rugged known.

The gold rush in the Tujunga canyons began well before the great California Gold Rush in the Sierra Nevada Mother Lode. The first settlers in the canyons, according to local historian Sarah Lombard, were the miners, who thoroughly explored the canyons of the San Gabriel Mountains. Several mines were located in those mountains and were worked for varying lengths of time.

Prospectors and miners wandered into the canyons and over the hills during the 1800s. Loggers cut the pines in the higher canyons for timber to shore up mine tunnels. The lower canyons were denuded of pine, spruce, and hemlock for wood to burn in the brick kilns of Los Angeles. Two major canyons were part of the land grant: Big Tujunga and Little Tujunga. Little Tujunga Canyon borders the western boundary of the rancho and is the most direct route over the mountains into Antelope Valley and the desert. Big Tujunga is a maze of canyons, tributaries, and rugged mountain terrain.

It was in 1865 that rich gold-bearing quartz was discovered in Little Tujunga Canyon. During the early 1870s, mines were tunneled into the hillsides, tools such as arrastres for crushing ore were built, and men panning for gold lined the Big Tujunga River and its tributaries. In the late 1880s, a minor gold rush occurred in the Big Tujunga. Small amounts of Placer gold were found in the upper canyons and along some streams.

A PROSPECTOR AND HIS MULES. Prospectors and miners were the first to enter the canyons, especially when gold was discovered.

THE SAN GABRIEL MOUNTAINS. Settlers were drawn by the beauty of the land. Surrounded by the San Gabriel Mountains, watered by a year-round river, offered a bounty of wild game, and promised a good climate, the Tujunga Valley was a natural magnet for those looking for a new start.

Mines, such as the Josephine, the Tujunga, the Hope, and several smaller diggings, flourished. The richest were the El Dorado and the Monte Cristo which, according to the many estimates, yielded anywhere from $70,000 to perhaps as much as $200,000.

By 1870, the territory had been overrun by squatters. By 1928, the richest of the gold ore was gone and mining continued on a smaller scale. During the 1930s, some families lived on the gold panned from the Big Tujunga River.

In 1850, pioneers began to move into the new state of California, the 31st state of the Union. The introduction of the American legal system was accompanied by simultaneous repeal of most Mexican statutes. A Board of Land Commissioners confirmed 521 of the Mexican land grants, but rejected some claims. It was difficult for the rancho owners to provide necessary proof of ownership. Several factors were involved: many of the owners of the ranchos had created movable boundaries with no recorded titles; land sales and trades were arbitrary; and the legal costs of confirming ownership were too high for the owners to legally fight to keep their land.

The demand for hides and tallow, the primary cash income of the Californios, was by then dominated by outsiders. The ranchos' wealth was drained off by foreign traders. They were rich in livestock and land and had an abundance of cheap labor, but they had not established a cash society.

The drought of 1862 to 1863 did more to hinder the ranches than all other factors combined. Cattle died by the thousands, while the grasses turned brown and brittle, dried up, and blew away. That catastrophe wiped out at one stroke as much as 25 percent of the state's wealth of actual cattle and cattle-related industries. At the same time, in 1863, a required $2 poll tax for each man aged 21-50 was instituted.

The Rancho Tujunga land grant, by that time, had been traded in parts many times over. Five years after the grant was confirmed, the Lopez brothers traded the Rancho "Tejunga" to Miguel Triunfo, a former San Fernando Mission Native American, for the Rancho Cahuenga, which was closer to Los Angeles. From that time on, the land has been traded, bought in parcels, subdivided, and finally annexed, in 1932, to the city of Los Angeles. The Lopez grant, however, was not lost or sold for debt as many ranches were.

The rancho to the east was Rancho San Rafael, close to the San Gabriel Mission. Jose Maria Verdugo claimed that piece of land in the late 1700s as a Spanish grant. The mountain range known as the Verdugo Hills borders Sunland-Tujunga on the south.

The canyons and mountains, during the late 1850s, were also used as refuge and hideout for cattle rustlers and horse thieves. Stolen animals were driven up canyons and hidden on the fine pasture lands of places like Chilao, Horse Flats, and Barley Flat. One such famous bandit was Tiburcio Vasquez. With his men, he drove the stolen animals up "Horsethief Trail" into the Big Tujunga Canyon to Alder Creek, then on up to Chilao and beyond. From there, the trails led into the desert. Along the way was water, grass, and shade in the many side canyons. Vasquez covered a great amount of territory with refuge: hidden trails, boulders to hide in, and good grazing.

There were times when the sheriff nearly caught up with Vasquez. Sheriff Thompson, with posse, recovered 150 horses in Big Tujunga Canyon and more in the Sierra Madre Mountains, but the bandits themselves were not found.

Vasquez felt he had good reason for doing what he was doing. The gringos in the north, where he grew up, had leveled too many insults against his Hispanic culture. He had some kind of idea that he could help Mexico regain California. For about 20 years, from 1852 until his capture in 1874, he and his gang terrorized Anglos in southern California.

His career came to an end when, in the spring of 1874, he and his men raided the ranch of Alexander Repetto. The outlaws tied Repetto to a tree and forced him to write a check for $800. They sent Repetto's young nephew into Los Angles to cash it. The boy acted nervous when he tried to cash the check and the bank manager suspected foul play. The sheriff was alerted. A half-hour before the posse arrived, the boy presented Vasquez with the cash. The posse followed, but stirred up a bit too much dust. The outlaws saw the lawmen's approach and the gang rode north to the mountains.

A rough, partially finished wagon road called the Soledad Turnpike wound up into the forest and lead up into Dark Canyon. It continued to the top of the divide separating the Arroyo Seco and Big Tujunga watersheds. The badly overgrown road ended and the gang, and the posse as well, rode into darkness on a moonless night. Both groups made camp, the posse at road's end and Vasquez and his men in a grassy shelter.

The chase began again at daylight. John Robinson, author of *The San Gabriels,* tells the story:

> The bandits reached trail's end on the crest of the divide, then plunged down through dense chaparral toward the bend of Big Tujunga visible far below. About two-thirds of the way down this thorny maze, just below what is today called Grizzly Flat, Vasquez's horse stumbled into a steep gully and broke a leg.
>
> The bandit chief was able to leap off the animal as it was falling and avoided injury. Vasquez reluctantly shot the wounded animal and continued downward on foot, carrying his saddle and two guns.

Vasquez thrashed through the thick brush, tossed aside his saddle and one gun, and hitched a ride with another gang member.

By the time Sheriff Rowland and his men struggled up the divide, they could barely see the outlaws through the thick, high chaparral and they were out of rifle range. By the time the posse had backtracked, Vasquez had vanished once again. Robinson continues his story:

A TYPICAL CANYON HIDEOUT ON HORSETHIEF TRAIL. Vasquez and other bandits followed this route because of water and lush grazing spots in the side canyons.

SISTER ELSIE'S WELL. It is said that Sister Elsie, a kind woman who dedicated herself to the care and education of Native American children, offered her well to drovers for the watering of their stock. This well was preserved and declared a California landmark by the Glendale Parlor of the Native Sons and Daughters of the Golden West in 1930.

> But time was running out on Vasquez. He made a fatal mistake when he did not flee to Mexico, as his friends urged him to do, or hole up in the unknown (to the lawmen) heart of the San Gabriels. Instead he hid out at Creek George's Ranch below Caheunga Pass . . . and was finally captured on May 14, 1874.

Vasquez had been convicted of having killed a man many years before in a barroom fight, as well as raiding and robbing. On March 19, 1875, in San Jose, California, Tiburcio Vasquez, bandit and folk hero, calmly met his death by hanging. So calm was he that he posed for a photographic portrait while awaiting execution. To remember the man who was so notorious, there are at least two places bearing his name: Vasquez Rocks above Soledad Canyon and Vasquez Canyon near Dark Canyon, the place where the sheriff almost caught him after the Repetto robbery.

Back in the 1850s, drovers watered their sheep at a well that had been dug by Mission Native American neophytes. The padres stopped there for water as they went back and forth along the Old Mission Trail. The place was well known as a welcome and refreshing oasis between the San Gabriel and San Fernando Missions, and was located in what became the Begue orchard in Tujunga.

It was believed that the well, by then named "Sister Elsie's Well," had been used by the Sisters of Charity of the Catholic Church. The church, it was said, had sent six nuns to Tujunga from the pueblo in Los Angeles *c.* 1850. The story at that time was that a Sister Elsie watered the herds of cattle at the well as they were being driven to the orphanage that she operated, which was there for the Native American children of Los Angeles County. Elsie directed the herding of cattle and other livestock and the planting of orchards, taught the children, and directed a dispensary for Native Americans. When Sister Elsie was troubled, she would look up to the nearby mountain peak to gain new strength and courage for her demanding life. "Sister Elsie's Peak" is said to have been named for her. In a quiet moment, one may stand on Tujunga Canyon Boulevard, once known as Horsethief Trail, look to the south, and imagine the sound of goat bells where Sister Elsie once lived.

There is a mystery still to be solved about the identity of Sister Elsie. It was found by historian Viola Carlson that there never was a Sister Elsie in the Sisters of Charity. She may have been from a different order or perhaps the kind woman was merely called "Sister." Maybe she was a nurse. Truth is elusive. History is ever-changing as new data is added. Today, there is "Sister Elsie's Well," still a landmark in Tujunga, and "Sister Elsie Drive," but the mountain was renamed in 1918 and is now Mount Lukens. Whoever she was, Sister Elsie and the outlaw Tiburcio Vasquez may have come face-to-face at the watering hole on Horsethief Trail where Elsie kept her cattle, goats, and gardens. On May 11, 1930, the Glendale Parlor of the Native Sons and Daughters of the Golden West decided to preserve the old well as a California landmark.

The Mexican period in California was short-lived, lasting only until 1848. Americans had begun to come into California in the 1820s, gradually marrying into Californio families and obtaining a great deal of power. Politicians were looking at California as a possible state. By 1872, southern California's transition from a Mexican cattle frontier to an American Commonwealth was almost complete. The boom of the 1880s was the final step in the dissolution of the ranchos and the completion of the transition from rangeland to agricultural economy.

Later, Governor Pico made the San Fernando Mission his headquarters, as did Colonel Fremont. The buildings were sold by Pico just before the American occupation. The book *The California Mission* describes conditions as they were:

> In the turbulent days that followed the Mexican take-over of California, the San Fernando Mission became involved in the provincial power struggles. Governor Echeandia, imbued with the new liberalism in Mexico, endeavored to convince the Indians that they should be released from mission bondage, and he equipped a small army of liberated neophytes from the southern missions to fight against a rival claimant to the office of governor . . . a revolt that died out.
>
> Secularization was hard at San Gabriel . . . When, in 1843, the mission properties were returned to the Franciscans, nothing was left at San

Gabriel but ruined buildings and a group of half-starved Indians.

Pio Pico somehow possessed himself of all the mission properties, and just before his death he gave the mission buildings and immediate surroundings to two Americans in payment of a debt.

The church itself was never completely deserted. The Franciscan Padres remained and cared for the Native Americans that were left until 1852. Nevertheless, most of them drifted away, mainly to the pueblo of Los Angeles.

SAN FERNANDO MISSION. The mission, established in 1797, is in operation today in San Fernando, California as a parish church and visitor center.

2. THE BEGINNINGS OF SETTLEMENT

The land the American settlers came into had been well used and well treated. It was explored by the native people, cultivated by the Mission Padres, and developed by the Spanish and Mexican ranchers. The soil was rich and the climate excellent. When settlers came, the cost of acreage was cheap and access to The Pueblo in Los Angeles was possible in a day's ride.

It has been determined that the first settlers occupying the Rancho Tujunga lands were in the Big Tujunga Canyon. Pedro Ybarra came first as a prospector and soon filed a claim for use of water from the Big Tujunga River, followed by filing mining and homestead claims. Ybarra built a ranch along Horsethief Trail. He planted a vineyard and a fruit orchard *c.* 1880 on the land where he and his sons continued to live for more than 60 years.

Other canyon settlers were the Bilderbeck brothers, who built a cabin in the lower canyon in the late 1860s, only to be murdered in 1871. There was Peter Phillipi, who planted an olive grove and kept honeybees; Farmer Johnson who also had olives and bees; and John Bryant, who planted a fruit orchard in 1889.

Another early colorful character, a canyon dweller, was "Barefoot Tom" Lucas. He was a day ranger in the old San Gabriel Timberland Reserve. It is said that Lucas did not have a home of his own in Big Tujunga, but preferred to move from camp to camp, hunting and patrolling the mountains. He was noted for his skill in tracking down and killing grizzly bears and other animals, and he often visited camps or ranches with game, which he would trade for other food and for tobacco. He was described as a man usually dressed in deerskin, bearing a waist-long beard, and carrying a single-barrel shotgun.

Silas Hoyt appeared in the Big Tujunga around 1883. Hoyt built a crude cabin from stones and logs collected in the canyon. From John Robinson's *The San Gabriels* comes this story about Hoyt:

> His only companion was a big grey horse named Beelzebub (Prince of Devils), which he used for work about the ranch and to haul his rustic wagon to town—the latter an infrequent occurrence, since Hoyt strongly disliked the city. One of Beelzebub's chief tasks was drawing in whole tree trunks for use in the cabin fireplace. They were never cut to

SILAS HOYT. Hoyt arrived in Big Tujunga in about 1883 and settled in the canyon. He built a crude cabin of stones and logs that he collected.

length, but rolled and pulled in through the front door as they burned off in the fire.

Another settler, Dr. Homer Hansen, filed a homestead claim on 93 acres in 1909 and built a cabin near to Silas Hoyt's. In a few years, he erected a two-story lodge where he entertained celebrities and political officers. Robinson relates some tales about Homer Hanson:

> Homer A. Hansen first visited Big Tujunga Canyon in 1892 as a teenager. Later, as a young doctor, he camped under its oak and spruce trees whenever he could find the time. In the early 1900s, suffering from acute inflammatory rheumatism, the doctor was told he had no more than a year to live. He retired into the canyon, where the sunshine and pure mountain environment worked such wonders that he fully recovered.

Of interest is the interaction between Hoyt and Hansen. When Hansen returned from the east, where he had received his education, he settled in the canyon he had loved so well when he was a teenage wanderer. It was then that he came across Hoyt. It is said that, because of Hoyt's practice of burning tree trunks in a windowless cabin, his eyes were damaged. In addition, Hoyt's eyebrows had grown so long that they curled right into his eyes and onto his cheeks. Dr. Hansen applied salve and trimmed the brows, thus saving the old man's sight.

Saved inside a white envelope in the museum in Tujunga are some dried maidenhair ferns that came from the cave where Hansen married Marie A. Huber. The site chosen was naturally beautiful; the walls and roof were covered with the ferns. All the guests, clergy, and bridal party were on horseback. During an interview with Marie Hansen by Sarah Lombard several years ago, Marie remembered that there were 28 people in the party, all mounted. Since Dr. Hansen did not own 28 horses, he rented them from the film studios in nearby Hollywood.

One horse had been trained to lie down when touched at the shoulder with a heel. When one of the women accidentally touched the horse, he promptly lay down in the middle of a stream. His rider had to dismount, wade to the bank, and remount before the party could continue merrily on its way. On the way back to the lodge for the wedding breakfast, some of the horses took advantage of the inexperienced riders and started running. One of the other horses, stopping quickly, sent his rider over and into a sand bank head first. The wedding cave is now somewhere beneath the Big Tujunga Dam and the sprig of fern is all that is left of that day.

The western portion of the Rancho Tujunga lands was surveyed in 1907, platted by Hansen, and named "Hansen Heights." The name was changed later to Shadow Hills (a part of Sunland). The streets were named after members of Hansen's family.

HOMER HANSON. Dr. Homer Hanson, early canyon settler, checks a rain gauge.

In later years, the canyons were well known for the many lodges and weekend cabins. One famous rustic lodge, Wildwood, was a popular gathering place during prohibition. Local folklore tells us that the many party-goers came into the canyons where liquor flowed freely (when the sheriff was not around). The canyons were so far away from law and order that there were few worries of getting caught.

Many of the surrounding areas in the foothills were known far and wide as health areas. According to Dr. Charles C. Coghlan in an article written for *Coronet Magazine* in October 1952, there is a strange phenomenon in the valley. As Homer Hansen was returned to health in the canyon, so have others regained their health upon arrival to the area over the years. There are examples of men, women, and children who could barely breathe from the effects of asthma, but who became robust, healthy individuals almost overnight. The recovery for those with rheumatic conditions was equally as amazing. Many sanatoriums dotted the land. In one neighborhood, the citizens rallied to protest one "san," saying that the people housed there were a health threat to the citizens on that street.

According to the Coghlan article, the reason for such health benefits is the following:

> The real key to what causes the region's healthfulness is a matter of geography and geology. Ranged on the south are the Verdugo

HAND-DRAWN MAP BY GREG LARSON. Charles Coghlan determined the reason for the healing air of Sunland and Tujunga.

SUNLAND SANATORIUM. Through the years, the foothills were considered a healthy place to recuperate. There were several sanatoriums. This photo of the Sunland Sanatorium was taken in the 1940s. At one time, the building was owned by the Volunteers of America.

Mountains. On the north are the San Gabriels, which reach a peak further inland of more than 6,100 feet. On the northeast lies the Mojave Desert, and on the west swells the Pacific ocean. The floor of the pass between these two ranges, rent down the middle of Foothill Blvd., rises from the west like a gangplank to a top of 2,000 feet. This is reached just east of Tujunga. Then the floor drops abruptly back to lower levels.

The San Gabriels are of granite. This stone has a high capacity for storing heat from the sun, which, since the range parallels the sun's course, beats against the south slopes from morning to night. After sundown, ordinarily the worst time for the asthmatic because irritants in the atmosphere settle with cooling air, the heated granite keeps the air warm and rising, pulling out any mischief makers it may hold. This updraft along the San Gabriels is so pronounced that an asthma attack artificially induced here may clear up in 20 minutes—elsewhere the attack may hang on for 3 days. The continual purging of aerial contaminants, then, is manifestly what makes the difference for the asthmatic in the Tujunga area.

This is not a phenomenon known only to settlers. When the native peoples lived on the land, they considered "a plateau above the river" as a place of healing.

Over the years, many convalescent hospitals and sanatoriums flourished in Sunland and Tujunga. One facility, The Sunair Home and Hospital, a non-profit clinic and home, was a community-sponsored project in Tujunga. It was a 40-bed nursing home on a 19-acre plot, specially designed for asthmatic children. The home was maintained for many years, care given at no charge.

Not only did the canyon dwellers, wood cutters, prospectors, miners, and adventurers enter the canyons of the Rancho Tujunga lands, but government surveyors and map-makers came as well. It was not until 1853 that the San Gabriel Mountains were surveyed to find railroad routes. At that time, it was the Army Corps of Topographical Engineers that carried out the project. John Robinson also relates that the government survey parties which explored the mountains had to penetrate thick chaparral and climb steep terrain, following just the ridges. This country was little known, rugged, and dry.

While the surveyors climbed, they were loaded down with barometer, tripod, sextant, compass, botanical box, and water. There were frequent hardships of the job. While climbing a high peak, two of the party became lost. By the time they were found, one of the men was completely exhausted and insensible at the bottom of a deep ravine. The second man was also exhausted and barely able to drag himself along on his hands and knees. Both were near death; they had not tasted food or water for 43 hours.

One member of another party, a meteorologist, perished after becoming lost. Robinson wrote that, "He died of thirst and exhaustion while attempting another ascent of an unnamed peak in the San Gabriels."

The mountains are still fiercely rugged and dry with some inaccessible areas. The San Gabriels, geologically a new uplift, consist of badly faulted and broken rock. These mountains are continuing to rise at an alarming rate, according to scientists and verified by those who have experienced the earthquakes in recent history. Mountains now have names like Mount Gleason, Mount Disappointment, and Mount Lukens (once called Sister Elsie's Peak), and all are carefully mapped. Some of the canyons, in addition to Big Tujunga, are named Little Tujunga, Haines, Eby, Gold, Trail, and Blanchard. Many are named for the original owners or users.

Little Tujunga Canyon lies at the most westerly portion of the original rancho. The Watts family settled in 1886 on an oak-shaded area near Gold Creek in Little Tujunga Canyon. They lived in a small adobe, which is thought to be the original Lopez cattle station. The ranch was successful in producing fruit, vegetables, and livestock.

Another ranch, the Stunden, on 120 acres, was situated nearby. Much later, in 1916, the Stundens sold their ranch to Cecil B. DeMille, Hollywood film director. DeMille renamed the ranch "Paradise Ranch" and proceeded to increase its size to 300 acres. He then built a spacious and pretentious lodge for family and friends. The family house was built of native stone. The entrance to the ranch was entered through stone abutments with an iron gate attached, the very gate from the 1927 film *King of Kings*. A circus railroad car was used as a bridge over Alder Creek. Behind the ranch was a zoo of sorts, containing camels, zebras, several kinds of deer, and peacocks. A small vineyard produced wine. During the decades of the 1930s through the 1950s, DeMille entertained lavishly.

Since the days of the first canyon settlers, roads and two dams were built, the Angeles National Forest was designated, and flood control systems were established. In the Angeles National Forest, campgrounds are provided for the hundreds of people visiting from surrounding areas in Los Angeles, those who drive up into the canyons to cool off and wade in what was once a large, year-round river and is now just a small, seasonal stream.

Over 100 towns were platted in Los Angeles County from 1884 to 1888. A large number of these were "paper towns" advertised as real estate developments that soon vanished from the records. As the Mexican and Spanish ranchers lost their land for debt or taxes, boundaries were re-determined. Government map-makers and surveyors fought the terrain to begin to make some sense of it all.

In the valley of Monte Vista (Sunland), orchardists and bee-keepers settled. The rancho segments from east to west were called "Hansen Heights," "Tejunga Terrace," and "Monte Vista." The land higher up on the slopes, at one time called "Glorietta Heights," was later developed into the Little Lands Colony, which soon became the city of Tujunga. The area was sparsely settled and undeveloped. All the land but that on the slopes was used for farming.

The Southern Pacific, after completing its transcontinental railroad in 1876, had encouraged people to migrate westward into southern California. Speculators rushed in to make their fortunes. Advertising in the eastern states painted a picture of a Biblical land of plenty. Recreational activities began to be popular in the rugged mountains and canyons, bringing potential land owners. The Santa Fe Railroad, which opened later, competed for customers and the fares fell lower and lower

THE LOPEZ ADOBE. The structure was built to be a cattle station. It was situated in what is now Little Tujunga Canyon.

THE ROCKY LAND OF LITTLE LANDS. Settlers were discouraged when they tried to farm the land on the slopes of the Little Lands Colony in Tujunga. They learned that beneath the rocks are more rocks—and it's rocks all the way down. . . .

until Civil War veterans, visitors, adventurous types, those wishing for something better, the ill and infirm, and those who wanted another chance, began migrating by the thousands. The population multiplied from 5,000 to 100,000 in 20 years.

Potential land buyers would hear promises that in the spring could be seen a paradise of wildflowers in brilliant colors of lupine, poppies, wild mustard, and bore covering the meadows. A mantle of shrubs covered the valleys and low hills—manzanita, madrona, choke cherry, lilac, wild mahogany, and coffee berry.

The new arrivals were promised a handy year-round supply of water, a warm and sunny climate, good soil, plenty of wild game, mineral deposits, and a rich supply of sand and gravel; everything needed for a pioneer family was on the land or in it. Not discussed were rattlesnakes and scorpions, hot desert winds, drought, torrential rains, fire, flood, and earthquake. Winds often blew at 65 to 100 miles per hour. Three major earthquakes and several smaller ones had leveled buildings and raised the mountains. Fires burned sometimes for long periods. One fire burned in the San Gabriels from June to September in 1872, consuming 58,600 acres before burning itself out.

Yet, the people came and stayed. John Robinson's book *The San Gabriels* describes the setting:

> This is inviting country, and mankind, for various reasons, has long been attracted to it. Few mountain ranges on the continent have been so swarmed over, dug into and built upon as have been the San Gabriels.

The valleys too, with the scenery of the majestic mountains and rich resources, have been used and re-used, loved and toiled over for 150 years.

Despite the exaggerations of the promoters, settlers soon became discouraged and many left. Settlers arrived, but a promised railroad did not. Nevertheless, Monte Vista and the Tujunga Valley survived.

Many names come to mind when speaking of settlers of the late nineteenth century. The Johnsons came to the valley in the early 1880s to cut timber. Later, they homesteaded close to 200 acres in the canyon, planting vineyards and orchards, and keeping bees. The Ardizzone family and the McVines grew grapes. The Wrights and Adams grew olives. There were several pioneer families to whom Sunland-Tujunga gives respect for the work they did in building a town from the rough land. These people, the Johnsons, Rowleys, Fehlhabers, Begues, Adams, and all the others, are representative of the early settlers.

The Rowley family is one of the best known. In 1882, Loren T. Rowley and his brothers loaded a buckboard with a number of bee hives, drove through the washes and over the roads provided by the woodcutters, and found land to homestead in the hills near Tujunga. They established a home with the bees, a horse, and a tent. In addition to homesteading and farming, Loren Rowley established the first general store in Sunland, was the first postmaster, picking up the mail from the steam trains in Roscoe several miles away, and was the first forest ranger in the 1890s.

Mrs. Loren Rowley had grown up as one of the younger children in a family of boys. She was a teacher before she married Rowley. She secured a teaching position in her new home after the former teacher quit. The boys in the school were rough; some carried weapons like guns or knives and would wield them if the teacher attempted discipline. Needless to say, the first teacher quit halfway through the year. But Mrs. Rowley's father had been a sergeant in the Civil War and she knew from growing up how to handle such upstarts.

The first Rowley son, Eustace, is said to have been "probably the first white child" born in the valley. A second son, Robert, was born in 1898. He is known as "the boy who would tackle anything" and is part of the folklore of the area's tough, rugged individualists that are so impressive by today's standards.

The pioneer heritage shown by the example of both Rowley parents affected the young man deeply. Robert said the following in his memoirs:

> I grew up learning to determine what I wanted to do. I had to do chores, of course, but other than that I was turned loose, and nobody told me what I shouldn't do. If it was there to do, you went ahead and did it. I'd tackle anything.

This confident attitude propelled him, at a young age, into activities not allowed today. He further recounts the following:

> We had chickens. The coyotes would come right up in the yard in daylight to grab a chicken. We'd run for a shotgun and see if we could get the coyote before it could get out of sight. The coyotes had their den down in the wash. You could hear them howl every night.

(This is still true.)

Robert's first hunting trip shows his willingness to "tackle anything." He longed to go hunting, but was told that he could hunt only when he was big enough to hold a shotgun and shoot it without the gun kicking him over. He was 13 when he shot his first deer. The deer weighed about 125 pounds and he weighed about 120. When he got under the dead animal, he didn't understand why he couldn't move it. He dragged at it for quite a while until someone came along and helped him.

Young Robert was expected to earn his keep. There was a time, in 1906, when his father picked up mail from the steam trains at the Roscoe station. Rowley ferried hunters as well, picking them up from the train depot and taking them into town. The visitors would stay in the hotel, then Rowley would guide them about 8 miles up into Big Tujunga Canyon.

On one momentous day, a group of hunters was to be picked up from the canyon site and delivered to the railroad in time to catch the noon train. When that day came, Robert was told to hitch up the two-seated surrey with a one-horse rig and go pick them up. The water was pretty high in the river and the road was washed out, so it took some time to make about 13 or 14 crossings of the river.

The men were in a hurry to catch the train. Robert recounted the adventure:

> We whipped the horse up and the horse started to go over a very rough road. It wasn't long before a bolt came out of the front axle, allowing the horse and shafts to come free, pulling me out, over the front running board onto my face in the sand—I was still holding on to the lines. We got the bolt back in and the shafts connected up, started up again and the same thing occurred. By that time one of them said he would drive.
>
> I was very happy to let him because I was kind of bruised up. He drove for awhile until he was getting to be a good driver so he whipped the horse up, hit a bump and went over. After that he said I could drive and I drove.

During floods, Robert would go into the canyon to rescue people. It was not possible to go by carriage when the roads were washed out. He would ride a saddle horse and lead one or two other horses. Because of the spacing of the horses, it was hard to handle three of them, all in different positions, in the stream. His horse would be "pretty near swimming" in the middle of the river and having a hard time holding its footing. "If the other two horses pulled back, the horse I was riding would have been pulled under if I didn't let go of the rope." Robert learned to get a very long rope and move clear across himself before the others started out. "Whether they wanted to or not, I'd pull them through. I was about ten years old at the time."

Robert tells another story of his life as an early settler:

> Father would go in with the wagon to Los Angeles to bring the groceries in, stay overnight and come back the next day. Then he traded some land for a 1909 Cadillac to run the mail and to run the stage from Sunland to Roscoe. He couldn't fix the car. If anything happened to it, we would hitch a horse in front of it. I'd drive the horse and he'd steer the automobile and we'd pull it 10 miles to Burbank where they'd fix it. We'd tie the horse on back and he had to trot while we drove the automobile back home.
>
> I learned to repair the automobile; I got very ambitious and really worked at it. I used to stay up until midnight working on cars, going up where anyone was working on one to learn how. I did it all on my own.

The Rowley land is now subdivided into town lots with small homes. The beautiful stone home they built is still on Hillrose Street in Sunland.

THE ROWLEY HOME. *This early Sunland family built one of the first houses in Sunland using river rock and field stone.*

3. THE FATHERS OF PROGRESS

Three men were the predominant forces behind the first settlement, the Little Lands Colony, in Tujunga: Marshall Hartranft, land broker; William Smythe, organizer of utopian communities; and George Harris, builder. They were three men of like minds that set out to model a community in Tujunga on the ideas of a philosopher, Bolton Hall. Hall was a New York socialist whose books *A Little Land and a Living*, *Three Acres and Liberty*, and *Things As They Are* advocated a lifestyle of community and collectivity. These men were the founders of the colony and, therefore, founders of the town of Tujunga, making significant modifications and contributions to the community for many years.

By the time Marshall Valentine Hartranft (pronounced hart-raft) came to California, he had spent some time practicing home gardening and selling the produce, working in a nursery, then in a produce market. Using his childhood experience and knowledge, he started his own market. After the failure of that first business, he was known to have recited the jingle: "To grow crops to sell is to speculate like hell, but to grow crops to eat keeps you standing on both feet."

Hartranft came to Los Angeles in 1890 where he published an agricultural newspaper called *The Los Angeles Daily Fruit World*, a periodical that educated the fruit-growers of the community. In 1900, he published a magazine-type paper called *The Western Empire*, of which George Harris became the advertising editor. Hartranft then went into the business of promoting the sale of agricultural land and using *The Western Empire* magazine as a sales instrument.

He brought in The Western Empire group in 1910, then the "Little Lands Colony" three years later. The "Little Landers," property owners of that cooperative colony, were encouraged to build their houses, plant some seed, get some goats, chickens, and pigeons, and sit back and enjoy life. The advertising went something like this: "Bring a shovel and a sack of cement, building materials are on site. Plant mushrooms in your basement and by the time the roof is on your house there will be food for the table."

Hartranft believed that land had value only when people lived on it. He also thought that the safest foundation of security and independence was to own one's own land and home. Easterners and Midwesterners read his magazine and found their way west to settle.

Marshall Valentine Hartranft. Hartranft, a land broker, settled in Sunland on his "Lazy Lonesome Ranch" He, the businessman, with William Ellsworth Smythe, the philosopher, founded the Little Lands Colony in 1913.

Another dreamer, William Ellsworth Smythe, had already established colonies of gardeners and small farmers on virgin land in California. "A Little Land and a Living" was the slogan, a phrase thought to have been adopted from his teacher Bolton Hall.

In the foreword of his book *City Homes on Country Lanes*, Smythe, whose philosophy was the foundation of the Little Lands Colony, wrote these words: "I am an optimist. I believe the world is going to be a better world for our common humanity in the next decade—the next generation—the next century—than ever before in the long history of the race."

Smythe had been instrumental in forming other utopian communities before Tujunga. He continued his monologue:

> And I believe the next passion of mankind will be for the soil . . . But if there is to be a transition in the life of the land—if new forms of industry and society are to emerge—then this will be due to the fact that the old life on the land has failed, is breaking down, and is doomed to pass away.
>
> That is what I believe to be true. In saying so, I sound no note of pessimism, but rather the note of hope, of confidence, of boundless faith in what the future is to bring forth. I know the land is to be the healing and the saving of the people . . . there is no other refuge.
>
> But before we can build a new life we must clearly understand that the old life has failed, and why it has failed. Then we must proceed to discover the principles upon which the new and better life is to be

founded. In doing so, must we not inevitably draw nearer to the Divine Purpose in making the goodly earth and setting man in the midst of it? And shall we not thereby evolve the Spiritual Man of the Soil, who, conscious of his partnership with God, enters at last into his true dominion?

Smythe's book, published in 1921, inspired Marshall Hartranft to hire him in 1913 to help develop the Little Lands utopian venture.

It was Hartranft's plan to find land of 1,000 acres or more about 15 or 20 miles from a city. He acquired option on the land, then sold bonds used to buy it. Once the land was paid for, it was subdivided into small farms and a town site, roads were constructed, and water was provided (one acre sold for $300, nothing down, and $3 a month). The two men believed that anyone could be independent on a small acreage irrigated and lovingly farmed. In many ways, Hartranft's ideas about a little land and a living were like those of Smythe. The two men joined together in their business ventures. Smythe was the idealist of the two and Hartranft was the businessman who could make the ideas work.

Glorietta Heights, earlier platted by Dexter, King, and Gilbert in 1888, was the land Hartranft purchased. That subdivision became, in 1913, "Los Terrenitos" or "Little Lands." For the town site of the subdivision, Bolton Hall was built. The idea in the socialist-type communities, such as the Little Lands, was that all land would be privately owned and owner occupied. In addition to a water supply already completed, and a village hall built, a cooperative store would be provided

WILLIAM E. SMYTHE. Smythe was instrumental in setting up utopian communities in several places. He believed that when a water supply is provided, small farms on small acreage could supply the needs of a family with some produce left over to sell. With Hartranft and George Harris, Smythe started the Little Lands Colony in Tujunga in 1913.

and all utilities would be owned and operated by town residents. The land itself, they believed, would sustain a family of four. They would grow enough food for themselves and a small additional crop could be sold to buy other essentials. The town site in Tujunga was a logical place for such a colony because it was undeveloped, yet a day's journey from Los Angeles. The land was cheap and there was fishing and hunting, plus rock and cement for the building of houses.

Hartranft had moved into the valley in 1907 and was soon known by the name of "Uncle Marsh." His wife was called "Aunt Lou." Marsh's business associates called him "M.V." The Hartranfts lived in Sunland on the "Lazy Lonesome Ranch," so named because, in his words, "I'm lazy and my wife's lonesome." His love for the valley showed in the generosity he extended by giving land for churches, clubs, for the Cross of San Ysidro, and for the Hills of Peace Cemetery. He gave the land to the women for their Sunland and Tujunga Women's Clubs so they could organize and do all the good things he knew they would do. In 1924, he saw the need for a fire station, so he priced the land far below the appraised value, selling it to the citizens for $750.

Men of Hartranft's caliber were controversial. Some thought him an ogre, while some said he was a savior. His work in soil conservation, as an author, and in exploration of the growth of things made him popular. He ran for Congress twice, in 1932 and 1934, but did not succeed in gaining the office.

The framework of the Tujunga community was formed by this man and was built upon by all those who followed. The Little Lands Colony was made up of about 200 people when it began. Since the colony had been billed as "the healthiest spot in the world," the people drawn there were the old, the sick, and the poor. There was a vision of human cooperation and the call of a land which offers itself to the human spirit. For some, the idea of the utopian colony worked. For many, the life was too difficult. After digging the stones out of the ground and building their houses, they found themselves without ice, gas to cook with, or mail delivery. While livestock sickened, gophers and lizards thrived. Beneath the rocks were more rocks. Many gave up the good life.

Hartranft went on making improvements. He replaced his horse-and-buggy stage, which he had used to transport potential buyers, with his Buick pickup truck fitted for passengers. He piped water from Haines Canyon, built reservoirs, and generally aided the town to survive and prosper. Pine School was opened. In 1908, 22 residents, with contributions of $220, got together and founded the Sunland-Tujunga Telephone Company. The town was developing. Marshall Hartranft, wearing pince-nez spectacles and leather puttees on his legs, must have been colorful. He rode around town in a Studebaker sedan with disk wheels and balloon tires. He worked continuously until age 73, when he died while working hard at his desk.

Bill Scott, a columnist for the *Record Ledger*, and John Whelan, a historian, wrote about one of Tujunga's most interesting characters, George Washington Harris, the designer and builder of Bolton Hall. The phrases used to describe him were "eccentric," "town character," "complete individualist," "oddball," and "hell-raiser." John Whelan, an old-timer who knew Harris, remembers the familiar sight of Harris when the creative urge fell upon him:

> He had a hair-trigger temper, and the slightest miscalculation, or even innocent remark . . . would set him off with explosive results . . . especially true when he had taken on a bit too much of the blood of the grape.
>
> To say that he was eccentric begs the question. Eccentric he was, often to the amusement of many of the local folk who refused to take him seriously.

He often dressed in a pair of shorts that had been reduced from old work trousers. In that outfit, he walked through town, carrying a copy of the *Iliad* under his arm.

Harris had strong opinions which he set forth in news columns. He appeared several times on Los Angeles radio, lecturing on a wide variety of topics. He was an intelligent, well-read, and artistic man, who had more than his share of determination and self-confidence. After graduating as a teacher, he traveled all over the United States, but it was in Los Angeles that he felt at home, seeing it as a place of virtue and benevolent governing.

GEORGE HARRIS. Harris, self-styled "nature builder," was responsible for the unique designs of many structures in Sunland-Tujunga and the surrounding areas.

A GEORGE HARRIS ARBOR. Harris built according to the lines of nature with as little change as possible.

Harris was at his best as a promoter. He fit right in with Marshall Hartranft, who hired him to write promotional material in *The Western Empire*. He decided, however, to move on and do something meaningful with his life. From near his home in Tujunga, he found a pile of native brush from which he cut and selected branches. From these, he fashioned a rustic chair and table. The experience taught him something which he would follow through with, to adapt to the particular lines of the wood's own growing. This new interest was leading him to a career in artistic building.

Harris had no experience with tools or building, but, being George Harris, it made no matter. He kept making garden furniture until he had an acre lot almost covered with it. In his words, "I have proved to my satisfaction that doing the work beats all the schemes on earth . . . I will in the future do the thing which is real, that which pleases . . . and from now on I turn my back on the artificial, the sham, and the expected because it is the conventional."

He became famous for the design and construction of rock fireplaces, stone cottages, houses, walls, pergolas, fountains, waterfalls, and public buildings. Bolton Hall is perhaps the most distinguished and by far the best known. In promoting himself, Harris said, "I can build you anything . . . from a cuff button to a stone house. I'll build most anything you need in this life . . . and when you're dead, I'll build your tombstone." Also, "I'm probably the highest paid pick and shovel artist in the world."

BOLTON HALL. At one time, fountains were placed next to the road in front of the clubhouse, one for man and one for beast.

Never too humble, he added "I quit business, went to work with my hands, and in three years, with a pick and shovel, a crosscut saw and an axe, sent my name around the world! My art consists in . . . following the line of least resistance." He promoted his work by publishing in newspapers and by distributing pamphlets and brochures.

One of Harris's many philosophical statements was, "I have respect only for decency . . . whether it is in the possession of a hod-carrier or a billionaire . . . Cultivate decency . . . and respect only decency." That eccentric hell-raiser made a contribution that has lasted.

From the first, there was the need for a meeting house, so in April of 1913, Hartranft donated land for the construction of a building. Using rocks gathered from local hillsides and the Tujunga Wash, George Harris, "nature builder," and his crew designed the hall to harmonize with its setting in the rocky valleys beside the San Gabriel Mountains. The great fireplace inside resembles a natural precipice under which Native Americans might have built their fires. To perpetuate a harmless pun, the name given was "Bolton Hall Hall" (after Bolton Hall, the New York philosopher).

Bolton Hall was built, or "grew," from native fieldstone, selected and collected by Harris himself. The building was constructed almost without plans by Harris and a handful of young stone workers. The stately rock building, once known as "the clubhouse," is in use now, as it was originally, as a community meeting place. Inside the building today is the museum collection of the Little Landers Historical Society, representing the history of the people and places in what was once known as the Rancho Tujunga.

The clubhouse was the hub of community activities. There were town meetings, church services, socials, weddings, and dances. Local people formed an orchestra and their music was heard on Saturday nights from one end of the valley to the other. The town library, set up in the newly opened hall, was the second library in the San Fernando Valley. The building was once owned by the American Legion for a meeting hall, but, encouraged by an influx of new residents, town leaders gained incorporation for the city of Tujunga in 1925 and the building became an ideal place for a city hall.

In later years, all municipal services were housed in the Bolton Hall building, the new city hall. Many townspeople remember taking their children to the health department for inoculations. The Los Angeles Department of Building and Safety was a busy office. All city business was transacted in Bolton Hall, even to the addition of two jail cells purchased from the city of Glendale for $1 each.

At one time, a bell hung in the tower. It had rung out many times for the calls to school, to church, and in time of disaster. The hall was at least once used for a refuge during storm.

For 20 years, the building stood empty after the new municipal building was built on Foothill Boulevard in 1957. It was boarded up, the bell was removed, and vandals played in the jail cells. In 1959, the city planned to raze the building. It was then that local citizens, led by Roberta Stewart, began their struggle to save Bolton Hall. Through their tireless efforts, Bolton Hall was not only saved, but in April 1962, was declared the second City Historical Monument. Still, the future of the building was uncertain until the Little Landers, with assistance from other civic organizations, campaigned for the building and raised funds to restore it. With matching federal funds, and later with city funds, the building was restored and reopened in December 1980.

BOLTON HALL. In 1913, when settlers moved in to the Little Lands Colony, there was need for a meeting house. Field rock was hauled to the site and this stately building was erected.

4. SURVIVAL

It was early on a Friday morning, August 6, 1921, when Loren Rowley's water tank collapsed. That day, according to the *Glendale Evening News*, Rowley was awakened early, not yet knowing about his great loss until a neighbor came by to tell him. The terrible news was that he had lost $2,000 worth of water and storage.

The tank, of wooden construction, could not be saved. Once having a capacity of 5,000 gallons, built upon timber stilts about 20 feet from the ground, it collapsed under the pressure of so much water. That small reservoir was the source of water supply to about 30 families. Marshall Hartranft, his neighbor, came to the rescue by connecting his pipe with the Rowley line.

As people settled in the foothills in the late 1800s, they filed for water claims on their property. One of the first claims was in the Big Tujunga Canyon, according to Sarah Lombard, and was filed by two men, Reynolds and Morgan, in September of 1870. It included "the water rights located in Tujunga Canon, North of the North boundary line of the Rancho Tujunga." Other claims followed, such as that of Phillipi in 1875 "for domestic and agricultural purposes at my residence on the lands situated in its vicinity and claimed by me under the Possessory Act of the State aforesaid."

Page and Howe, after they filed claim to the waters of Big Tujunga Creek in 1883, created a water system for the village of Monte Vista, which started in Pipe Canyon. As more settlers came and claimed land, each also claimed the water, each then refining the flow of it. Charles Miller, a columnist for the *Record Ledger* and a local collector of oral histories, wrote in 1986 of the events of the time:

> Haines Canyon ran like creek the year round from springs at its head. Bluegum Canyon was gorged after heavy rains, but ordinarily was dry. Blanchard Canyon, the same. Zachau Canyon stood dry until rain water drained from the Seven Hills watershed above Tujunga. And the Tujunga Canyon Wash ran all year, alive with trout for the locals. . .
>
> In the first decade, the settlers carried by hand all water for their household needs or, until the first well was dug, fetched it up by mule team from the Wash.

THE WATERSHED OF BIG TUJUNGA CANYON. The canyon provided water for the valley and beyond. Land promoters boasted that the gallons of fresh water flowing into the Tujunga River were ten times greater than that in the surrounding canyons.

The question in the minds of the settlers was how to capture the water and get it where it was needed. Pioneers like Fred Petrotta had to carry water from a big, leaking water pipe leading to the Begue Ranch.

The watershed area for Sunland-Tujunga was (and is) large. Land promoters boasted that the gallons of fresh water once flowing into the Tujunga River were 10 times greater than that in the surrounding canyons.

The hauling and hefting was gradually replaced with small sand-bottomed reservoirs with pipes heading downhill from them. The intake area often had to be cleared out. By 1910, there was a genuine water company operated by local men in Monte Vista.

Meanwhile, on the rocky slopes of Tujunga, was the beginning of the planned community of Marshall Hartranft and William Smythe with water piped to every parcel of land. William Smythe was also considered a famous irrigation crusader. He wrote that water would become the elixir of social justice. Thanks to the irrigation ditch, he said, family farms would replace agricultural estates. According to Smythe, democratic opportunity had been stolen after the Gold Rush by overbearing land and railroad monopolies. In one of his statements, he claimed, "The reshaping of the state's hydrography has conjured cities out of the desert and put California fruit on the tables of the world."

In an effort to supply water for irrigation and domestic purposes, the people of Tujunga formed the Haines Canyon Water Company in 1910. At that time, the water supply came principally from two wells augmented by a gravity supply, with two concrete reservoirs (without roofs) and one large dirt reservoir, uncovered and unlined, just a hole in the ground. Charles Miller mentions that with the construction of the water boxes that trapped the Haines Canyon flow and settled the sand, the delivery system for the upper Tujunga was assured and Hartranft could be assured of water for his land.

It soon became apparent that the water company could not provide enough supply for the ever increasing population. More wells were dug and reservoirs were built. The location of one well in mid–valley had booster pumps to fill one reservoir. The pumped water from this well easily supplied the 5-, 10-, and 20-acre parcels of land just east of Mount Gleason Avenue and west to the olive and orange groves in Sunland. A second reservoir was built higher up.

It was not until 1928 when the Southern California Water Company took over operation. The first thing the company did was to thoroughly clean the two concrete reservoirs and construct permanent roofs over them. They then constructed the 750,000-gallon reinforced concrete reservoir on the high elevation just east of Haines Canyon Avenue in 1929. By 1949, the Southern California Water Company was serving the nearly 4,000 customers.

A few years ago, *The Green Verdugo Hills,* in an article by Mabel Hatch, an early Little Lands settler, recounted J.H. Livingston's expertise on the water problem:

> J.H. Livingston was one of the men in charge of the water system in those early days, and he tells of the many trials and tribulations of the job. Livingston reported: "The first pumps, it seems, hadn't the needed power and had to be torn out and bigger ones installed; when pumping was started to fill the reservoirs, redwood plugs were driven in to the ends of the laterals to keep the water climbing, but as soon as the water reached the first of the laterals, the plugs blew out and everything had to stop while the plugs were spiked in." When operations were started again, the spiked plugs held all right but the ones at the next level blew when they were reached and again time was called for more spiking; and so, with great difficulty, blowing plugs as it went, the water hobbled all the way to the reservoir. . .
>
> The next problem was for the man at the pumps to know when the reservoir was full, so the ingenious Mr. Livingston built a raft and floated it on the water in the reservoir. On the raft he put a red lantern—then he pumped until the welcome red glow of the lantern showed above the wall of the reservoir.

In spite of all these difficulties in its delivery, the cost of water was low, $1 per 1,000 feet of domestic water and 2.5¢ an inch per hour for irrigation water.

The Haines Canyon Water Company sold to the American States Water Company. In 1951, Los Angeles Water and Power bought out American States. Another reservoir was added and more pipes were added, bringing in other supplies of water. A basic staple was restored.

Agriculture was the chief occupation on the Rancho Tujunga land during the late 1800s and early 1900s. Orange groves had flourished on Mission lands, so the first settlers planted trees as early as 1846, some from cuttings of the Mission trees. Avocados were introduced in 1862. One early resident, Mr. Flory, had 135 plum trees on 1.5 acres in 1891, which produced 5,230 pounds of fruit. The prunes were sold for $523, while the production cost was only $18.

As early as 1880, the olive industry was prevalent in Sunland. The Wright brothers had brought in olive trees from the San Fernando Mission groves. By 1892, Alfred Adams Jr. had purchased the groves and the Adams Olive Cannery and had built up enough of an olive business to be able to haul his produce by wagon load to Los Angeles to be used in the "free lunch" served in saloons.

In the beginning, the cans were being sealed by hand. By 1915, the Sunland Olive Company had expanded enough to purchase a mechanical can sealer. They were also able to purchase a truck that doubled as a freight service and tourist bus. By 1916, the olive crop was expected to yield about 150 tons. Three years later, the cannery employed 25 people for the canning season. By 1924, the cannery was the largest employer in town, employing 20 men and 30 women at $800 a week. The olive company proved to be the most visible and successful agricultural enterprise in the area. During the years of World War I, Adams Olive Cannery was processing peaches, apricots, and tomatoes for the military.

In 1923, a carload of canned apricots and three carloads of ripe olives were shipped to England. Each can was plainly marked "Sunland." Each year was more

FARMING LAND. In the rich land around the river, crops of every kind, including olives, oranges, prunes, and avocados were successfully grown.

successful—30,000 cans doubled the 1922 olive output, then 1,455 cases were shipped to New York by boat and 3 carloads were shipped to Boston, then on to Hawaii and Alaska until, in 1936, giant green olives were shipped to the Vice President in Washington, DC. The next season, the White House ordered a case of "giant greens."

One of the workers in the Adams Olive Cannery was Marion Johnson, daughter of early settler Cornelius Johnson. In her own words, she tells us the following:

> There used to be lots of olive trees all around here, but by the 30's the cannery had grown so much they were going clear up to Porterville, getting olives and trucking them down. Your black olive would be picked fairly green. And picked green, they were very hard.
>
> At the cannery they would put these green olives in big vats and put lye water on them for a while. The lye would take the bitterness out of them and turn them black. You have to take the lye out of them, so you put them in clear water for a while. Then you'd put salt brine on them to make them tasty, palatable. You have to keep changing the water and brine solution. That all would take about three weeks.
>
> The women didn't work with the lye; the men did that. The women started in with the sorting; my first job in the cannery was sorting. They'd bring them in big buckets and put them on a wood tray that had

ADAMS OLIVE CANNERY. At the cannery, the fruit was put into large vats of lye water. Then, to remove the lye, the olives were stored in clear water for awhile and later soaked in brine. Women did the sorting.

ADAMS OLIVE CANNERY. As the town's leading industry, the cannery was at one time the major employer for the local citizens. The company opened in 1891 and closed in 1955.

a board across the bottom of it. We'd roll them, sort them, and if there were any soft ones we'd pull those out. When we got all the fruit sorted, we'd open this board and they'd go on a conveyor belt down to be put in a box.

They'd take that box into another room which had sinks; the olives would be washed with water and put into cans . . . I was the one that put them into cans. I did all the jobs. Part of the time I was the one that took these trays of cans and put them by the capping machine which sealed the cans with lids.

Later I was on the capping machine, putting the olives on the machine. You'd put them on four cans at a time, and the four would go around and be capped. Just before they were capped, this hot salt brine would fill them. A man was on the other side of it controlling the brine flow. Then the olives had to be cooked.

I wasn't making much money. Even working in 1950 you were making pretty good money if you made $1 an hour. There is a standing joke: get somebody to eat the olive off the tree, because they're the bitterest things you'll ever taste.

It was an article from July 14, 1955 in the *Record Ledger* newspaper that told the rest of the cannery's story:

Historic Adams Olive Cannery is torn down to make way for a 34 home tract. Another landmark passed from the Sunland scene Tuesday, when workmen began to tear down the historic Adams Olive Cannery at Sherman Grove Avenue and Wentworth.

On its site 34 three and four bedroom homes will be erected by Caltura Builders, Inc. Though the cannery was a frame building, its demolition posed one major problem—the removal of the stone pits for the pickling of olives, some of them as much as 15 feet deep.

Founded in 1891 by Alfred Adams, Jr., the cannery brought prominence to Sunland through the worldwide distribution of Sunland and Monte Vista canned olives . . . Title stamps on the deed indicated a purchase price of $40,000 . . . homes will be in the $13,000 to $14,000 class.

Excerpts from the *Record Ledger* show other agricultural successes: "In 1929, Cacti plus 200 varieties of fruit were growing on a 2-acre lot in Sunland and an exceptionally large grape crop was reported."

Grape vineyards stretched from Sunland to the end of Tujunga. That year, the return on grapes was $400 an acre. A new variety of tomato weighing 1.25 pounds was grown. Mountain cling peaches, developed and grown only in Sunland, were in great demand.

Big Tujunga Canyon and the San Gabriel Mountain gold mines yielded one kind of gold. There was another gold, however, which profited more. California discovered a source of wealth 20 years after the 1849 gold rush in the state. That gold, the symbol of prosperity, elegance, comfort, and luxury, was in the form of oranges. From the 1870s to the 1930s, citrus farming was a $2-billion industry.

The transcontinental railroad was responsible for this great boom, making it possible to carry fruit from coastal cities and the inland valleys to the East Coast, even to Queen Victoria in London. Thousands came to establish themselves as gentleman farmers, since cultivating the citrus groves could be easy, very profitable, and even dignified. What was once a luxury soon became a staple of the American diet. In Sunland and Tujunga, orange groves patterned the landscape. Nearby La Tuna Canyon was once named Orange Cove.

By 1894, citrus farming was extraordinarily profitable in southern California. By 1903, oranges were bringing great wealth to the entire state. Nearby Pasadena was the site of an Indiana colony devoted to raising oranges. It is not by chance that Orange Grove was called "millionaire row."

In the mid–eighteenth century, orange cultivation began at the missions. Four hundred seedling trees were planted at the San Gabriel Mission in 1804 from cuttings brought from Spain by Franciscans. The first commercial plot was a small one in Los Angeles. The orange empire of southern California began declining during the Depression. After the post-World War II population boom, the groves began disappearing as land became more valuable for housing and industrial development.

In the valley, there had been 2,200 people in Sunland operating truck farms, flower fields, grape vineyards, strawberry fields, fruit trees, and olive and orange groves. Eggs were a cash crop. Goats were prolific and raised for milk. Chicken and turkey farms flourished, as well as rabbits for meat. A eucalyptus industry was started to grow trees that would quickly provide lumber for the promised railroad. In Hansen Heights, a butterfly farm shipped rare species all over the world and raised local insects for sale. There are still remnants around town of eucalyptus and olive groves, with old citrus trees still bearing fruit, and an occasional thick-trunked grape vine.

Religious services were an important part of life outside of work. In the days of settlement, the churches were places of worship, gathering places for fellowship, and a nucleus for planned recreation. Near the town park and the lake, and a large pasture where the people gathered on Saturday evening for square dancing, there was a Free Methodist Church. The pastor was James T. Wornom.

"He's comin'!" "Parson's comin' home!" Men would stop to listen. Women would pause. They all knew what the song meant. The parson was on his way home after a spell of preaching. In the valley, sound could be heard from miles away. It is said that the sound of evening laughter bounced from rock to rock and a cough could be heard for miles. It's no wonder then that the song of the parson was an event for pause.

Historian Viola Carlson wrote that old-timers remembered sleeping outdoors on cots on hot summer nights. Far down the valley as the parson's covered wagon crested the western hills, they would hear the clop-clop of horses' hooves as James and Jenny Wornom returned from one of their preaching trips. Ringing out strong and clear would be the voice of the preacher singing, "Lord I'm Coming

TURKEY FARM. Poultry farming was one of the most successful and lucrative of the cash crops.

Home Never More to Roam." The parson's wife, affectionately called "Aunt Jenny," would accompany him at church services by playing a small pump organ that could be carried on their wagon.

Wornom was one of 14 children and the son of an itinerant preacher. His family had been known for their singing ability. The settlers affectionately called him "The Old Parson." He was a big, rawboned, blustery sort of man who was full of his religion, who lived religion, breathed it, sang of it, and preached it. For a time, he preached in the church that stood in the Sunland square. Usually, however, he preached from his covered wagon, accompanied by his wife who played as he conducted the singing.

During the week, the parson would draw fertilizer and leaf mold for his neighbor's gardens or lend a hand to build a house or to dig a cesspool. Never was there a family in the valley in trouble that Wornom was not available to assist.

Wornom told friends that because he loved these hills so much, he wished to be buried in them. He asked Marshall Hartranft, his good friend, for help. "Marsh," he said, "You've always promised me the land for a cemetery so I could be buried in these hills. Now I'm getting ready to leave and I haven't got it." The parson was more than 80 years old. He was tired.

After he became ill, Hartranft, though he took his time, finally selected a site of about 4 acres in the foothills and sent his laborers to make a road around the main hill. When the site was ready and the road completed, he went to see his friend. "I have your cemetery now, Parson," he said. It is said that the next day, the parson died, as though he had been waiting for his cemetery. The town gave him "the swellest funeral you ever saw."

PARSON JAMES WORNOM AND HIS WIFE JENNY. *Parson Wornom was an itinerant preacher. With his wife, he drove their small wagon out to remote areas. On it was a small pump organ that "Aunt Jenny" played for the singing of hymns.*

PARSON WORNOM'S FUNERAL PROCESSION. The funeral was said to be the "swellest funeral in the world." The buggy went as far as the narrowing of the trail. The parson's casket was passed hand over hand up the new trail.

The report of the funeral took up most of a page of the *Los Angeles Times* on April 24, 1922. The headlines were: "Loved Character Borne At Last To Rest" and "Sunland Neighbors Bury Preacher On Mountain . . ." The *Times* reporter's article included the following:

> The Parson Of The Green Verdugo Hills, well known by reputation and by the reporting of him by John S. McGroarty's page in the *Los Angeles Times* . . . died in his home in Tujunga.
> The neighbors turned out and spent three strenuous days making a winding trail to a high hill at the foot of the mountains overlooking the vast sweep of the San Fernando Valley. He sleeps now where he often sat astride his horse looking across the valley to the Ventura Mountains and the Calabassas Road. The funeral was a picturesque pageant and of a character never witnessed in these modern times.

The article describes the procession. The body was driven in the parson's old house wagon on which he and Aunt Jenny, who still survived him, had made innumerable journeys to camp meetings. At the foot of the winding trail, the neighbors took the coffin from the wagon and bore it on their shoulders to its last resting place under the glow of the great mountains.

The funeral was replete with military honors, since Parson Wornom had fought in the Civil War, "in which he bore himself gallantly." The men carried the coffin in relays along the steep winding trail. A long procession followed, preceded by a

WEIMAN CHURCH, 1922. This beautiful church was one of the many stone buildings in the area.

squad of the American Legion, who fired a parting volley from their rifles over the grave. Two buglers, one at the grave and one on a distant hilltop, sounded "Taps."

His grave marker reads: "First Grave at Hills of Peace 4/22/1922; Rev. James Wornom Parson of Verdugo Hills." Jenny was buried beside him in the graveyard located on the street now called Parson's Trail.

Anna Barclay writes in her diary about the "Singing Parson," whose hale, hearty voice and his "God Bless You" reverberated throughout the valley, as did his singing of songs such as "It Is Well With My Soul." In a quotation from her diary, Barclay related her enjoyment of the parson: "In the little church just through the park, which is quite clearly visible from my window here, the Singing Parson held services as he has held them for lo! These many years."

Sometimes, the pioneers were reluctant to turn out for worship, but it is related that Parson Wornom used to start ringing the church bell and kept ringing it until a congregation gathered.

The history of the First Baptist Church in Sunland begins in July of 1908. A group of 29 people met at the home of Edgar Lancaster to organize a Sunday school for the neighborhood children. The Sunday school that had been meeting at the Lancaster home had become too large. They met then at the Sunland schoolhouse until, again, the group outgrew the building. According to Paul Lancaster, "My father, Edgar F. Lancaster, founded the first church because my brother Bill and I refused to go to church with girls." So, the Sunday school for boys began in the front room of the Lancaster home with a group that grew and soon outgrew their surroundings.

In November 1910, a meeting was held at the schoolhouse to officially organize a Baptist church. By 1913, the group, again needing larger quarters, bought the building of the Free Methodists in Sunland Park, the same location as the first church in Sunland. By 1923, another structure was built closer to the main part of town.

The Church of the Ascension in Tujunga was an Episcopal Mission church started in 1914 from the Saint Marks Episcopal Church in Glendale. Before the church building existed, services were held in member's homes and several times in Bolton Hall. It was in 1917 that the Church of the Ascension was erected, the first church to be built in Tujunga.

Our Lady of Lourdes Catholic Church followed in the same manner. Members first met at the home of Mary Forester in Tujunga, where services were held by Father Joseph Tonello in the family living room. The first of these masses was delivered on October 17, 1920. The people had previously attended services in La Crescenta, conducted by father Quetue, a former missionary to Africa.

There have been many additions to the church population and many changes since 1938. A long list of priests, pastors, rabbis, and lay people have come and gone, each leaving a legacy dedicated to the area's spiritual life.

SUNLAND BAPTIST CHURCH. *The church was founded by Edgar Lancaster, who gave a parcel of land on which the church was built. This 1912 Sunday school class was mostly girls.*

5. A Town of Character

History belongs to those who photograph it. There is a collection of photographs taken when the towns of Tujunga and Sunland were just getting started. There are probably few communities whose beginnings have been so thoroughly recorded pictorially. Valuable information about the buildings, scenes, and people are gratefully cared for at the museum. It is due to the work of Joseph Lamson that this photographic view of the community is possible.

Joseph (J. Harry) and Alice Lamson arrived in the area in 1910, where Lamson began to photograph almost everything there was to photograph. In truth, he moved away from Los Angeles to Greeley Avenue in Tujunga to build a business free of competitors. He also wanted to handle all business alone with only the help of his wife. Lamson was attracted to the Little Landers community, of only about 30 families at the time, and their ideas.

When the Lamsons arrived in Tujunga, they pitched a tent on a site purchased from Hartranft. They did not know a thing about carpentry, but they worked together, learned as they went, and built themselves a home. They used eucalyptus poles for the rafters, Tujunga Wash sand for mortar mix, and built a stone fireplace using field rock. They built the windows of photographic glass plates cleaned by an acid bath. Alice built a stone patio all on her own. One room became Lamson's studio. Their home was comfortable, friendly, cool, and shaded by oak trees. It was considered by the community to be a true work of art.

Lamson began by photographing residents, finally amassing hundreds of portraits. He photographed weddings and took children's school pictures. He carefully marked each of his photos in the corner with his signature and sometimes the date, which has and will continue to be invaluable to researchers looking into the early history of the community. Besides his work in photography, he helped Hartranft by selling real estate.

Lamson's collected photographs contain all the town "firsts"—the first fire station, the construction and dedication of Bolton Hall, the old Tujunga Valley Bank, and theaters. He took pictures of waterways and scenes of floods and snow storms and people. He served as the official photographer to Poet Laureate of California John S. McGroarty. His wife was a color artist and worked with her husband throughout the years. Lamson was an invaluable asset to the community.

Harry Lamson's home. Lamson and his wife Alice, though untrained in construction methods, built their own home. The windows are made of cleaned photographic glass plates. Alice built a stone patio by herself. Lamson, a photographer, is responsible for a pictorial history of Sunland and Tujunga.

Penny Terry was born in 1913, the same year that Bolton Hall was built and the Little Landers settlement began. She was a woman who, as a part of a pioneer family, helped build the town. Her family lived on the upper end of Valmont (the address then was 732 east El Centro) with 17 other families.

Charles G. Cleveland Terry, Penny's father, was a fine stone mason. In a photograph, he stands outside a stone building holding a specialized rake. C.G.C. Terry had determined that the way he was mixing cement was not as efficient as it could be. An inventor as well as stone mason, he created a rake which had holes in the tines so that a small stream of water could come out into the mortar mix.

Penny reports that it was her father who built the magnificent fireplace in Bolton Hall under the direction of George Harris. Harris, she said, took all the credit, but her father and other stone masons did the work on the building. After the Hall became a clubhouse, she did not visit it often. There was no time for that sort of social life for the Terry family. However, she does remember once seeing that the young men, trying to impress the young women, would bring lemons to throw into the light fixtures in the clubhouse.

Some canceled checks give an idea of the cost of the Terry family items and income. Check number 13, dated June 9, 1923, is to Penny herself: Pay to the order of Penelope Terry $1, signed by her mother Nella Terry. Other checks are made out, in amounts of $1 or $2.50, to the Mr. Bangs Store. Most food was grown by the settlers, but Bangs sold other goods and Phillip Reihm sold meat.

Life at home could be difficult. One unforgettable adventure occurred when a bear ripped into the shed. Also, there was the time, as a child, when Penny went under the house to gather eggs, but as soon as she reached for one, something whipped out and grabbed her. It was a rattlesnake that had latched on to the heavy curls of her hair. She backed out quickly and the snake let go, not having a firm hold. Her mother ran, got the shotgun, and made quick work of the snake. Penny, at 86, can still see the sight of the snake's belly in front of her eyes.

Chan Livingston came to Tujunga with his family in 1910 at the age of 12. He has fond memories of the recreational activities in the town. He was 16 when he played in what he called "the first big game" on July 4, 1914.

In a speech given to a Little Landers group a few years ago, Livingston told the fascinating story:

> The summer of 1914 our first baseball team was organized. Baseball talk had been a topic of conversation at the croquet court and horse shoe pitching pit in Sunland.
>
> Eustice Rowley and I between us were able to come up with two bats and two well used scratched balls that had at one time been the property of Glendale and San Fernando High Schools. It was immediately

PENNY TERRY. She is shown here standing on a typical Tujunga rock wall c. 1923.

obvious that the playing conditions of the pasture presented problems. Due to cow droppings, cattle foot prints and in general the unevenness of the field, it did however, provide an excuse for the constant errors made by the self-imagined super stars.

The community had definitely become baseball-minded, with talk of Ty Cobb, LaJoy, Honus Wagner, Tris Speaker, Three Finger Brown, Christy Mathewson, John McGraw, Connie Mack, and the famous double-play combination of Evers to Tinker and Chance. A newcomer from the East by the name of Harry Tidebole had been a spectator at many major league games. His tales and talk aroused the desire and stimulated the "self-imagined super star" qualities of his listeners.

Thus, the plans to organize a local team soon became a reality. Bill Graham agreed to be the manager. There weren't many young men, but when all noses were counted, Graham had a team of just nine to put out on the field. Bill permitted the boys to pick their best playing positions, although there was one complication that popped up: a fellow named Brick White informed Graham that unless he could become pitcher, he would refuse to play. Brick became Sunland-Tujunga's first baseball pitcher with little dispute.

Bob Freeman and Harry Grosvenor were the tallest men on the team. Grosvenor said he'd played first base in Vermont. Coupled with the fact that he owned a glove, he became first baseman. Livingston remembers how the team started out:

> As for myself, I had now played for two years on the Glendale High School team. E. Rowley had also been a team player on the San Fernando High School team. Rowley and I were the two kids on the team while the others were in their middle twenties. Difficulties cropped up when Bill Graham got us all together for our first practice session. There were only six players who owned a fielders glove and no catchers equipment.

They built a crude backstop in Rowley's cow pasture at the spot now at the corner of Fenwick and Floralita (across from the Monte Vista Hotel at the time). Gunny sacks were filled with sand to be used as bases. Home base was a board painted white.

There were two fellows, Earl Holcom and Eddie Gilmocker, who worked in Los Angeles as steel workers. They owned a Model-T Ford and would return home on weekends where they lived in a house tent. Since they were both top wage-earners, they agreed to purchase the catchers equipment, plus two bats and one new ball. They were reimbursed later from the voluntary hat-passing.

The Sunland-Tujunga team was dressed in the uniform of the work-day clothes: most wore bib overalls and work shoes. About 50 spectators came by Model T, horse cart, or on foot to see the community's first big competitive exhibition. Livingston tells the story:

It soon became obvious that the one and only ball would become an irritating factor. When a foul ball was hit past the back stop, or to the left or right side of the field, the game would be at a standstill until the ball was recovered. These delays aggravated the visiting team. Their constant scurrilous remarks to the local spectators, who quickly classified them as enemy number one, were soon returning remarks. Before the sixth inning, two fist fights had erupted which also delayed the game. Probably fifteen errors were committed by our club.

Our team was at bat in the 6th inning. A foul ball landed in the weeds in left field. Those loyal spectators, and a dog that had been chasing and returning the one and only ball, found themselves outrun this time by the dog. Two days later the ball was found in the yard of the owner of the dog. The umpire called the game as completed. The final score was: visitors—21. Sunland-Tujunga—2.

Two other games were scheduled after the Fourth of July in 1914. In the following two games, the town was clobbered in excess of ten runs per game.

A fourth game had been scheduled; however, the visiting team failed to show up.

Mabel Hatch was an early settler who recorded her memories. She once wrote that it would be impossible to put on paper the hopes, fears, frustrations, tragedy, and comedy that stalked over the rocky hillsides in the early days. She points out that we all owe a lot to the men who dug the rocks and the women who worked by their sides.

When they stepped off the dingy old train at Roscoe station, Hatch and her father, a Civil War veteran, fully realized that they had left behind forever the green hills of Michigan. They stood on the edge of the dry and rocky land they had bought. Hatch's father was 70 years old by then and his experience had been in business and politics, not farming. They had come to the valley hoping that his health would improve in a friendlier climate where he could garden and find some peace.

What they saw was neither friendly nor peaceful "It was the roughest, toughest looking piece of land I ever saw." They went ahead and settled down, since they knew they were stuck with the land. The Hatch family learned to love it, even though there were stones and more stones. By the time they had their shack built, the advertising promises of "deep yellow sunshine" had turned a burning yellow and not so friendly. They would go faithfully to the town meeting at the clubhouse and discuss with their neighbors the problems and solutions they had discovered. Hatch described the people that had joined them in the first meeting after they bought their land:

> I looked round at the people in the audience. Next to me was a woman
> of 50 or so, perhaps more, with a tired, lined face but with the look of

fearful eagerness in her pale eyes. Her hands were smooth and well-kept. She was a stenographer or office worker or maybe a teacher. I noticed how tightly she clutched her bag, a worn, black leather affair . . . next to her were a heavy red-faced farmer and his frail, frightened-looking wife.

He, too, was reaching for the money bag hung around his neck.

There were small businessmen who had developed asthma and needed a better climate, as well as widows, spinsters, and bachelors, who had just begun to realize that they had better fasten on to something after the roving life. Hatch remembers, "There were all sorts, but a few things they had in common; mostly they were middle aged or older . . . and had taken a beating from life and now, with a last throw, looked and hoped so eagerly for a new chance."

The women who settled were a special kind. One, Cora Bel Linaberry, built her home and called it "Bird's Acre," her mission being to feed the wild birds. Marie Frisch, born in Austria, and Anna Souto, born in the Azores, lived on their 1.5-acre plot. They built their own walls and chicken coops and successfully raised as many as 1,500 chickens. They also raised kale and alfalfa for chicken feed.

Chan Livingston praised his mother for her endurance as she kept house in a tent infested with red ants: "I remember how my mother accepted and adjusted to the situation . . . with stability and courage."

MARIE FRISCH AND ANNA SOUTO. These pioneering women bought land when the colony was first started. They built their own chicken coops and their own walls and, eventually, had a ranch with 1,500 chickens, which they fed from the alfalfa and kale that they grew.

It was the women of the town that eventually formed the groups that enhanced the community through the Tujunga and Sunland Women's Clubs, social and church groups, and the many groups that added stability to the difficult work of making a living.

The story of Cornelius Johnson and his victory over the "last Los Angeles grizzly" is an integral part of Sunland and Tujunga folklore. Johnson, kin to the Johnsons who homesteaded in the 1880s in Tujunga Canyon, produced honey, fruit, and wine to support his family, as well as to carry on the Johnson family tradition. An article by Peter Hess called "Cornelius and the Grizzly" brought his tale into a new focus:

> On Sunday, October 22, 1916, Mr. Johnson and his wife were walking in the rugged ravine about a half mile east of their lower Tujunga Canyon home when Mrs. Johnson spotted some animal prints in the soft earth. She thought they resembled elephant tracks, but Mr. Johnson knew immediately that a bear had left them although there had been no signs of bears in the area for many years.
>
> The tracks made him uneasy. A hungry marauder could raise all kinds of havoc in the apiaries the family kept . . . and the orchards and vineyards which were just coming into their peak. But what really concerned Mr. Johnson was the safety of his seven-year-old daughter, Lucille, who had to walk to the Sunland elementary school every morning.

THE DEMISE OF THE GRIZZLY. *The celebration of the last grizzly's death ended with a bear barbecue in the park.*

Home in the hills. A ranch house in the Big Tujunga Canyon.

Two days later Johnson purchased a 15-pound Newhouse No. 5 bear trap, which he situated in an irrigation ditch and baited it with a piece of stale beef . . . He lashed the trap to a 50-pound sycamore log. On the night of the 27th the trap closed on the grizzly's foreleg. The following morning, Johnson followed a trail of thrashed bush a half-mile up the mountainside where he found the exhausted animal, the log having snagged in a thicket of bushes. Taking aim with his .30 Marlin rifle, he killed the bear with one shot behind the ear.

Johnson chained the carcass to a pole and four neighbors helped him carry the bear off the mountain. At the local butcher shop the mature female bear weighed in at a scant 256 pounds . . . she was skinned, butchered and the meat either given or sold to the neighbors, some of it consumed later that evening at a communal barbeque. The old-timers liked it, but Cornelius Johnson himself judged the meat too "fevered" to eat and buried the remains near his house.

The "Sunland Grizzly" and the photograph of Johnson with his foot on the carcass became legendary—a certified icon, the last of its kind, a victory of man over nature's adversity.

The controversy was, and now remains, about the classification of the bear, referred to as a silver-tipped. Was it really a grizzly? Was it really a southern California native? It seems that the skull of the bear did not match that of California grizzlies.

In a letter to zoo director Joseph Grinnell from an Elmer Belt in 1939, it was suggested that the "Sunland Grizzly" had escaped from the Los Angeles Zoo in

Griffith Park. The zoo keepers were anxious that the public not know about any escaped bear, nor about a possible release of animals from the zoo, so the story was kept a secret. The zoo at that time was small; just a menagerie of livestock, wolves, monkeys, cats, an aviary, and a few bears in hillside caves. It was an enterprise facing big problems. Hess reports on the state of the facility:

> Critics didn't like the cramped, unnatural settings and some small animals were known to have escaped . . . the health department was threatening action over zoo sewage draining into the Los Angeles River.
>
> It isn't difficult to envision a grizzly making her escape from such an environment. She may have followed the Los Angeles river (which would remain unchanneled for two more decades) flowing past Griffith Park through Glendale and Burbank to its Tujunga tributary. It isn't even much of a stretch to consider that a foundering zoo facing a budget crunch, possible relocation, and impending meat rationing might be tempted to release one or more of its denizens into a nearly native and sparsely populated canyon habitat.

Johnson did not know of any of these matters, but was told much later. Whether or not it was the last of the California grizzlies, he did see the threat to his home, his livelihood, and his child.

The 1920s town of Tujunga had a doctor. Gladys Maygrove's memoir includes a story about the town "Doc" who lived in Tujunga in the early days (beginning in 1913). In a community of about 200 people, there would not be much in the way of a medical clinic, but there was "Old Doc Carney." Doc was a kind man, Maygrove writes, with many professions. First and foremost, he was the shoe repair man on Commerce Avenue. He was also the part-time minister, one of the trustees on the school board, and, in a pinch, his shoe shop was an emergency first aid center. Maygrove wrote the following:

> This brings vividly to my mind the time I was pushing my little sister Bing in a wheel barrow. The roads were rough and bumpy . . . as I was trying to run with my "passenger" she fell out of the wheel barrow, almost biting off the tip of her tongue!

The girls' mother heard the scream and came running. Bing's mouth was full of blood and tears. Maygrove tells how Doc made it all better:

> My poor mother gathered up the injured party and half running and walking took off for Doc Carney!! We had no phones in those days and we lived at the end of San Ysidro Street.
>
> With a bath towel draped across my sister's mouth we reached the shoe repair shop. Doc Carney was repairing a pair of boots. He gave one

look at my sister, wiped his dirty hands on his leather apron and proceeded to take over. He stuffed what looked like the insides of her tongue back in place, put a clamp or some such thing over the ripped tongue and told her in quite a matter-of-fact way, "keep your mouth shut." No antiseptics, no washing of the hands, he just got busy . . . and it didn't cost a cent!

Maygrove told of another night:

> We were playing for the Saturday night dance. I felt a headache coming on, possibly from reading too much music. Mr. Hartranft was there. He came over to me and said he could help my headache. With his forefinger and thumb he pinched gently in the corners of my eyes and held for a few seconds, then repeated the same . . . my headache was relieved.
>
> We didn't carry such a thing as a headache pill in our purse in those days, and my mother didn't have her "smelling salts" with her for me to use.
>
> I wonder how many remember the old smelling salts bottle . . . usually a small green bottle and was so strong one's eye would water after taking a sniff.

Another old-fashioned remedy she mentioned was the use of a slab of hot bacon rind placed on the chest for a cold. And in the summer time, always a big pitcher of cream of tartar to "clear the blood."

Tools of the Trade. Some of the equipment used by doctors and chemists in Doc Carney's time included the scales, mortar and pestle, and homeopathic medicines.

Many years ago, on Shady Grove Avenue in one of the oldest houses in Tujunga, lived a remarkable and well-liked fellow, Arthur "Slim" Vaughn. He had been a valley resident since 1916.

Vaughn was a true character of the "real old west," renowned the world over as the "Southwest Tumbleweed" for his 500 poems and short stories. According to Vaughn's memoirs, he was the first Western cowboy to appear in full regalia on television. He called himself cowboy-adventurer-poet, detailing quite a life with his burro and dog, plus the buzzards, coyotes, rattlers, scorpions, and Gila monsters of the deserts.

For over 25 years, Vaughn followed the covered wagon trails and the pony express routes, as well as the locations of old mines and their tailings. He would cover as much as 1,000 miles on a trip, living a rugged life in the "vastness of the merciless sun-scorched deserts" of the West.

In town here, some of us remember a more settled Slim. A familiar sight around town was his old truck labeled "All American" Landscape Business. The truck was often loaded with youngsters squealing with delight as he took them for short rides. An article written about him features him as Santa with a hearty crowd of kids out to meet him. Santa arrived in a helicopter that year (1967).

He was considered the most colorful man in town. With his flowing beard of magnificent proportions and luxuriant shoulder-length hair, he was downright

ARTHUR "SLIM" VAUGHN. Known as the "Southwest Tumbleweed," Slim was a colorful member of the citizenry. He worked some of the time as a cowboy at Knott's Berry Farm in Buena Park.

A CLEAN-SHAVEN SLIM. The whole town showed up to see Slim's face. He agreed to the shaving of his beard when he became engaged to a young model.

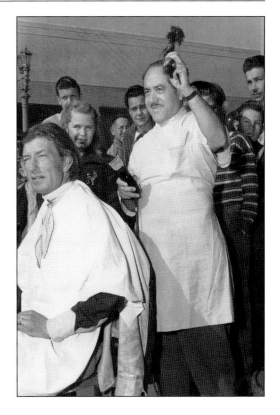

handsome. At least one March, in honor of St. Patrick's Day, Vaughn dyed his greying beard green.

Aleene Mallette wrote a tribute to Vaughn in the *Record Ledger* in March 1968:

> Intensely patriotic, when World War Two broke out, painted his truck red, white and blue, and on V-Day, with a load of shouting children he tore up and down Commerce Avenue and Foothill Boulevard through Tujunga and Sunland off and on all day shooting blank cartridges into the air to celebrate the victory.

During the years that he lived in town, he worked at the landscaping business, was an actor portraying western characters in films, and was an entertainer at Knott's Berry Farm. He was the model for the prospector on the Knott's billboards. Slim appeared in parades all over the country and everywhere he went, he lauded Tujunga.

At one time, as a young fellow in 1947, he became engaged to a young model. As a stipulation of the engagement, he had his hair cut and his beard shaved off. It was done in full view of everyone in a barber chair on the street at the corner of Tujunga Canyon Boulevard and Commerce Avenue. After the engagement was broken, he let his hair grow back, never to be cut again.

It was in 1960 that he had another experience involving his beard. He said, "I was just getting ready to whip up a mess of vittles and the danged oven blew up. Thought for sure my beard was gone. Was so glad to find it was only singed that I didn't even care about the two windows that got blown out." The loss of the beard was a pretty serious matter. "It's part of my character. Guess I should have it insured."

Vaughn was not only the planter of lawns, builder of stone patios, tree surgeon, actor, poet, chauffeur for such as Tom Mix and the like, but was also a perennial candidate for Honorary Mayor of Sunland-Tujunga. He finally attained the office in 1958 when Los Angeles mayor Norris Paulson bestowed that honor on him. Vaughn bore the position of mayor proudly when doing official duties, always wearing a top hat and cut-away with black tie, and often a fresh flower in his lapel.

He was only 63 years old when he died of a heart ailment. It was said that many missed his cheery smile and the wave of the hand of the roving ambassador of good will, the man with the greenest thumb in town, a man full of love. The "Southwest Tumbleweed" is remembered as a man who raised high the proud banner of rugged individualism. He was an individualist without being an iconoclast. His self-reliant eccentricities gave the community some of its individualism, character and personality.

SLIM AT WORK. Vaughn acted as a gunfighter for visitors to Knott's Berry Farm in Buena Vista.

6. Sunland: The Beautiful Vale of Monte Vista

Across the highway from the Monte Vista Park, to the south, was the acreage of another settler. William Bernhard, German born, fled from his native land across the Isthmus of Panama *c.* 1865 and settled in Napato to escape conscription in Bismark's army. However, in 1875, Bernhard left Napa and came to Sunland. Phil Begue, another pioneer who had a farm near Tujunga Canyon and Foothill, used to say that Bernhard moved into Sunland when the Native Americans moved out.

Bernhard made a living with bees and honey until, in 1884, he purchased 80 acres west of Newhome Street for $1,000—$100 down and the balance on contract. He planted grapes and peaches. As early as 1890, reports tell us that Bernhard's crop, grown on 10 acres, produced 25 tons of fruit, including peaches, grapes, berries, apricots, and prunes. That year's crop sold for $750; the cost of production was $70; and the net profit was $680. In addition, the area was described as "soil, heavy loam, not irrigated, vines 5 years old."

The only reason Ted Bernhard, William's Napa nephew, came to Sunland the first time was to give his Uncle William help in the vineyards and peach orchards during the harvest season. William Bernhard's home was on Oro Vista and Wyngate Streets. Only six families lived in Sunland in 1899. Ted Bernhard, already a successful young businessman in northern California and one of the wealthiest men in the state, first set foot on his uncle's ranch in that year. After that visit, he traveled the Southern Pacific many times to Los Angeles, then rode a horse and buggy to Sunland. On his way home to Napa after the visit in Sunland, he would drive down Sunland Boulevard to the Roscoe station at San Fernando Road and flag the train.

As the years went by, Ted Bernhard came south more and more often until, in 1934, his uncle died at the age of 90. By then, William Bernhard owned 200 acres of choice land in Sunland and, being a bachelor, his estate was divided between Ted and his brothers and sisters.

Ted Bernhard was already established in a series of enterprises: grocery, the baking and meat businesses, meat slaughtering and shipping, cattle raising and brokerage, and land purchasing. He was a shrewd investor in stocks and bonds, as

THE BEAUTIFUL VALE OF MONTE VISTA. *John Steven McGroarty made the "Beautiful Vale of Monte Vista" well known through his articles in the* Los Angeles Times *and* Trails Magazine.

well as an oil company. In 1902, at the age of 22, he became a director of the Crescent Petroleum Company located in Maricopa, California. About his wealth, Bernhard once said, "Being in the 80-90 percent income tax bracket is as high as I want to go." Perhaps he was ready to settle down in Sunland.

At the time of one report in 1956, Ted Bernhard was an active man of 76 who owned nearly 80 acres of land in Sunland and lived in a large, handsome hill-top home. At that time, he lived a quiet life in which he was primarily involved with the Sunland-Tujunga Telephone Company. He was the primary stockholder. He described himself as an active man, "too active worrying about the country's ills. The country's drunk with too much prosperity," he declared. "Taxes are getting out of hand and prices are too high."

The property that was once Bernhard's has yielded to many homes, mainly developed as apartments and condos, looking at the same mountains and at the same Sunland Park as Uncle William and Theodore did those many years ago.

John Steven McGroarty arrived in town as a visitor in 1915. As an author, his writing shows a romantic sensitivity. In *Trails Magazine,* he wrote a description of Monte Vista as he saw it:

> I was saying that a man misses a good deal by sticking so closely around
> Los Angeles all the time . . . the Valley of Monte Vista lies only fifteen
> miles through the gaps of the hills through Los Angeles.

Monte Vista? Ah, here was a new one. The wanderlust was upon me at the mere mention of its name . . . I spent one whole day of glory there . . . I saw a vale that day as fair as any in all the Land of Heart's Desire.

Every wild thing that grows and every wild bird that sings are there. The chaparral that I crushed beneath my feet filled my nostrils with perfume. I followed trails the which to pass I had to part the wild rose vines in twain. The wild grape hung above me, the music of the singing waters was in my ears. It was a valley of canyon-indented hills, little dream canyons numberless, and the great Tejunga at the end leaping from the campagna away into the heart of the mountains. And I found people there, quaint and lovable people there . . . and there were live oaks.

In the 1880s, the settlers in the foothills and plains of the local area had admired the great stands of oaks. Advertising for the Monte Vista Valley bragged of their beauty. In 1887, the "health community" of the Monte Vista Valley was advertised as the gem of the mountains, boasting of the splendid Monte Vista Hotel and magnificent oak groves, saying, "If any of the trees are as old as people say, some of the local trees were around when the first pilgrims arrived in America."

Sherman Page, a lawyer, and F.C. Howes of Los Angeles purchased 2,000 acres of the 6,660.71 acres of the Tujunga Rancho in 1883. They started the village of

OAK TREES IN SUNLAND PARK. *The oaks are important to the environment in the hot foothill areas, providing shade. Many oaks live 1,500 years and have a root system of as many as 100 miles. Acorns from one oak could provide food for a small hunter-gatherer family for one year.*

Monte Vista, a parcel of 40 acres of prime land, and subdivided it into tracts of 10 or more acres.

The first water claim in Monte Vista was made in 1870. Page and Howes filed the claim in 1883 and brought in a 10-inch pipeline for water. The 40 acres was platted for the town and the remaining prime land was used for farming. By 1885, there were 23 families living in Monte Vista and 200 acres under cultivation. Some of the early settlers were the Adams family, Sidney Jumps, John Kirkness, Frank Barclay, and the Blumfields.

Barclay built a grand and elegant hotel, the Monte Vista, and began a land-selling enterprise. A smaller hotel, the Park Hotel, was built first for the purpose of housing hunters, vacationers, and land buyers while the grand Monte Vista Hotel was being constructed. After the visitors disembarked at the Roscoe station, they would either walk or take a conveyance of some kind driven by locals. Near a beautiful stand of live oaks, they would arrive at one of the hotels. The grand Monte Vista Hotel was advertised as the place where potential land buyers could stay for $4 a night while they investigated the surrounding area.

Unfortunately, Barclay bought and developed the hotel at the end of the land boom, went broke, and lost it. Dr. Q. Rowley bought the building as an investment and the luxurious place enjoyed great popularity. As the years went by, the building went through several sales and was used as a home for undernourished children, a home for the elderly, and in its later years, as Cyprus

MONTE VISTA HOTEL. *The elegant hotel was built to lure the wealthy to enjoy the beautiful valley of Monte Vista. Opened in 1887, the resort offered the most modern amenities.*

Manor rest home. The home closed in 1959 and the building was demolished in 1964. The small Park Hotel building survived until the 1971 earthquake, after which it had to be torn down.

Large-scale advertising brought people up the winding, dusty roads from Los Angeles by way of Glendale. Others came into the Roscoe station on the steam trains and made their way through what is now Sunland Boulevard, then a rutted trail. Many bought land sight-unseen as they viewed the beautiful landscape from the hotel.

The advertisers for Monte Vista offered an all expenses paid package for the prospective buyers. The fares would be deducted from the selling price of the land.

People who arrived in the Los Angeles environs found local hills covered with oaks, poppies, walnut trees, and willows. Sunland itself was planned around the grove of oaks that became Sunland Park. The oak is especially important to the environment as a shade tree in the hot foothill areas. Oaks grow to an elevation of 3,000 feet, usually in groves of 25 to 75 trees. The height of a mature oak is 35 to 65 feet and it is often 75 feet broad, providing a great amount of shade. Many oaks live 1,500 years and have as much as 100 miles of roots in their system.

Timothy Turner, who wrote an article for the *Los Angeles Times* called "Sunland Park Live Oaks Popular for Picnics," pointed to the artistic form and growth of the oak, describing the trees as "gnarled, twisted fellows, growing so close that the light of day finds it hard to struggle through them down to the ground. One group of these trees, specially old ones, have large limbs which have reached down until they touch the ground and grow along it."

These words describe the oaks in Sunland Park as the settlers saw them. Children enjoyed climbing on them and picnickers came by the thousands. Flappers danced beneath the moon on a huge dance floor up the highway at the Garden of the Moon and under oaks in Kagel Canyon. It was under an oak that the *Record Ledger* newspaper was born, the office of the newspaper on a table beneath a tree. A dense grove hid many a bootlegger's still during prohibition.

We blame mankind for decimation of natural growth, but nature sometimes deals a blow. In the 1940s, oak leaf gallflies invaded the area and Sunland Park was never again the same. Pine trees were planted to replace the dead oaks. John Whelan, Tujunga resident since 1920 and local historian, and Tom Theobold, also resident since 1920 and former postmaster, suggested that the diversion of the underground water for flood control, along with the trampling down of the soil around the trees, made it impossible for them to get the water to nourish that giant root system.

One oak can take up as much room as a house. Sometimes, the big trees get in the way. There is a particularly poignant story of a family striving to save one old oak, most of which was on their property. A builder needed more clearance for his driveway, so he decided to chop down the tree probably existent since the times of the hunter-gatherers. The tree, though guarded by family members and lamented by the neighbors, was felled and a nice, straight driveway took its place.

SUNLAND PARK. This beautiful stretch of park land was called a "renowned mountain valley park." It was the centerpiece of the village of Monte Vista.

All this tearing out is such a reversal of the earlier sentiment. There was such fame from these local trees that, in 1929, and with great pride, 25,000 seedling oaks were taken from the Sunland Park grove for propagation at the Los Angeles park department at Griffith park. The stands of oaks still survive in some places along the canyons where there is underground water.

Sunland Park itself is a place taken for granted in Sunland and Tujunga, and in adjacent communities as well. It is a busy place all the time. The town of Monte Vista was built around it; it seems to have always been here.

An 1887 advertisement for the "health community of Monte Vista" read that an excursion led by Bartlett's Seventh Infantry Band would open up "Magnificent Monte Vista," the "Gem of the Mountains," the "Queen of the Valley," 1,500 feet above sea level, 20 miles north of Los Angeles, with a splendid hotel and magnificent oak groves. Sunland Park was in the center of the original 40 acres of the village called Monte Vista. "Judge" Page purchased the land and set it aside as a public retreat in 1884. Known once as Tejunga Park, then Monte Vista Park, the place was dedicated in perpetuity for Page by his daughter.

A chamber of commerce magazine, dated 1947, acclaimed:

> At the turn of the century, when Sunland was known as the town of Monte Vista, the frontier stage coaches stopped just around the corner from the heart of Sunland's renowned mountain valley park. Imagine, if you can, the surprising paradox of Coney Island Ferris Wheels . . . red caramel apples . . . games of skill . . . amid the picturesque setting of 700 year old oaks and a matchless panorama of mountain scenery.

The picture of those days is a peaceful one. Lancaster Lake and the park were close together. The church and a school were adjacent to the park, as well as a hotel, small stores, cabins, and farm homes. Twenty-three families lived in the village with 250 acres of fine land under cultivation. There was sweet water, wild game in the hills, and a marvelous climate. A short walk took one to the river where swimming holes had been dug out. People helped each other in work and enjoyed each other in play. They had to. They needed each other.

Through the years, improvements were made to the park grounds and problems were solved. For instance, something was amiss in 1915; tree surgery was needed for the oaks and additional upkeep was petitioned for the park. As many as 39 oak trees were bought at $200 each. The county forester was uncertain of the exact boundaries and the area had to be surveyed before adding land to the grounds. Over six acres were purchased and permission was granted for concessions to operate outside park boundaries.

In August of 1915, the Ladies Aid Society of Sunland had a large stone oven built in Sunland Park. The next ice cream social was improved by having a fire to huddle around while eating ice cream. Two years later, two more furnaces were built. There appeared a new challenge. Quite a few campers were setting up tents and there seemed to be no legal way to evict them. The year 1918 brought 250 newly planted trees to the park, a contract set to clear the grapevines away, and an ice cream stand installed under the oaks.

The park in Monte Vista had become a popular place for many communities, as evidenced by the great numbers of people holding large gatherings there. The Teacher's Federation picnicked and a Los Angeles firm brought 125 employees.

AMUSEMENT RIDES IN SUNLAND PARK. "Imagine, if you can, the paradox of Coney Island Ferris Wheels . . . red caramel apples . . . games of skill . . . amid the picturesque setting of 700 year oaks and a matchless panorama of mountain scenery."

Over the years, Easter and Fourth of July celebrations drew large crowds. The carpenters union brought 200 people and the Bible Institute came with 300. The Kansas State picnic welcomed 150, while the Kiwanis of San Fernando chapters came by the thousands. Union Oil Company visited and thousands arrived for Memorial Day.

By the 1920s, there were swings for the children's playground, a restroom for the ladies and concrete picnic tables. In 1920, *Mark of Zorro* was filmed in the park, starring Douglas Fairbanks Sr. In 1929, a stucco building was installed for a night watchman to live in. More restrooms were added, in addition to shower and locker rooms.

Though changed over the years, Sunland Park is still the community's valued place for rest and recreation. There are several baseball diamonds, two recreation buildings, play areas, handball and basketball courts, tennis courts, a rollerblade rink, many tables, and plans for a skateboard park.

Meanwhile, on the lower end of the valley, land formerly belonging to Homer Hansen was being developed. Once known as Hansen Heights, the area now called Shadow Hills occupies the western portion of the old Rancho Tujunga. The present-day uniqueness of Shadow Hills is due to its low-density housing,

STARR VON FLUSS'S "SHADOW HILLS." Then, and still, Shadow Hills is an equestrian community with homes on large parcels of land. It was so loved by some of its inhabitants that this music was written about it in 1950.

OLD VIENNA RESTAURANT IN SHADOW HILLS. On the western part of the old rancho is the portion once called Hansen Heights, now Shadow Hills. The Old Vienna Restaurant, still in operation, was completed in 1937 and built by August Furst.

ranches, equestrian emphasis, and the efforts of its residents to maintain a place where the land and nature take precedence over development.

Over the years, specialized businesses have been built in Shadow Hills. There was the Butterfly Park where, as early as 1929, for a $5 per year membership, a person was entitled to 1-dozen mounted butterflies, admission to an enclosure where thousands of butterflies were raised in their natural state, and admission to its museum. The ad says: "To reach Butterfly Park take road connecting Roscoe and Sunland to Hansen Heights Store, turn south two blocks."

Amos and Ardeth Ikenberry owned a large orange grove along Sunland Boulevard during the 1940s. As Amos sold oranges from a stand on the road, he came up with the idea of making orange cones and slush drinks. From this came the "Famous Amos" frosty business, which he sold later to Jimmy Dean's.

Old Vienna Restaurant, also located on Sunland Boulevard, carries a story of its own. Old Vienna Gardens was built by August Furst, from Nuremberg, Germany, to be completed in 1937. The gardens became a popular place to dine and dance outdoors in the perfect storybook setting. Tudor–style lines set with boulders make up the main structure with lovely stone work surrounding the property. There are complex terraces and canals. It is known now as the Villa Cinzano.

Above the restaurant is the Moorish–style residence built by Furst in 1936. Many rumors have been attached to this home. It is said that in it are secret and hidden places. Also, a rumor circulates that German spies once stayed there and that there was once an infamous Hollywood brothel held there. Whether or not these stories are true, it remains that the home and grounds are old and very beautiful, situated in a wonderful, scenic part of the country. Of particular interest is that Furst put his piping under the driveway to take advantage of "solar" heating.

Not far away is the lovely property once called "The Frog Jump," home of the Spence family. The Spences sold to a Catholic school. In later years, the building and grounds became the group home known today as Tierra del Sol.

The famous "Tommy Trojan" (Richard Saukko) of University of Southern California fame and his horses, Traveler I, II, and III, are noted among the more famous personalities originating in the area. The equestrian group "The Spirit of the West Riders" rode the Rose Parade in 1998. There are many others who have and are now contributing to the vital life of Shadow Hills. There is no place more peaceful and amenable to horse lovers, animal lovers, and country lovers than the one-and-only Shadow Hills, the rural area, the "country" within the city.

Shadow Hills is not the only rural mecca of the Los Angeles area. The northwestern portion of the Rancho Tujunga is now named Lake View Terrace, once called Tujunga Terrace. Located at the base of Little Tujunga Canyon, it is also rural in nature. It lies at the edge of Los Angeles, still in the city limits, and is adjacent to the San Fernando Valley.

This area developed as an agricultural outpost with fine soil for growing almost anything. In 1888, the Tujunga Terrace grammar school was built for the farming families. Almost immediately upon the founding of a village, a school was organized. The chronology of school for this area began in 1887 with the opening of Vinedale School in Orange Cove, adjacent to the rancho lands, with an enrollment of nine boys and five girls. The "Tuhunga" school district was established in 1888 in "Tejunga" Terrace (Lake View Terrace) in a one-room schoolhouse located in a field. The average daily attendance was 28 students. In 1895, the Monte Vista School (Sunland) was built, taking 11 students from Tejunga Terrace. One teacher taught all eight grades.

By 1900, Sunland School had one or two students in each grade and frequently none at all. During stormy weather, a small lake often surrounded the building and there would be no school that day. Hansen Heights (Shadow Hills) school was formed in 1912 and more schools followed. When Pinewood school began in Tujunga in 1935, a tent was used to house the students. In those years, the schools were a hub of community social activity.

Chan Livingston wrote: "In 1911, five of us boys became eligible for high school. Eustice and Robert Rowley commuted to San Fernando High School by a two-horse cart. A public bus system was in operation from Sunland to Glendale. It was a converted Buick wooden box body with two board seats running parallel. The Buick had no top."

Other students went to Glendale High. Two 1908 Cadillac sedans were provided for the school children and they had to hold on to the outside running boards because the full-fare, grown passengers had first priority to the seats. The old dirt road was dusty and bumpy. It was not until 1937 that Verdugo Hills High School opened in Tujunga.

At the 1988 reunion of the Tujunga Terrace grammar school, the list of alumni showed a hearty list of Japanese names: Akiyama, Higurashi, Tokashiki, Ohama, Tamori, Imai, Mitsui, Moto, Takeuchi, and others. Mabel Tsumori Abe, recounting her memories, said that the Japanese workers in Tujunga Terrace and Hansen Heights (Lake View Terrace and Shadow Hills) first arrived when a Norwegian Baptist lady from Roscoe (Sun Valley) hired two Japanese bachelors from San Francisco to help her with her property. They lived with her and did all the heavy work while she did the cooking and laundry, an amiable use of expertise.

As time went by, more Japanese settled there and became a basic part of the agricultural richness of the area. In a gully in Sunland, one farmer had a hog farm, while others grew vegetables, fruit, and flowers. Mabel Tsumori Abe remembered her job of watching her father's produce truck as he made his rounds. She said that during the hard times, especially during the Depression, people would steal food with little conscience. Her father would negotiate while she was on duty. He would bring a small bottle of wine from his friends the Ardizzones in Tujunga and some small tin cups. The men would imbibe a bit as they talked over the day's news. The bottles were always small enough to fit into Mr. Tsumori's front overall pocket.

SUNLAND SCHOOL. By 1900, Sunland School had one or two students in each grade, or frequently none at all, especially after rainstorms when the school yard became a small lake.

7. On the Upper Slopes of the Valley

The upper part of the rancho land, though not rich for agriculture, attracted other families. The Begues had come in the 1880s as bee keepers with a number of stands of bees. Philip Begue bought a little over 10 acres of land from V. Beaudry, then mayor of Los Angeles, paying $5 per acre for it. As reported by the *Record Ledger*, "For the first few years Mr. Begue's taxes on the whole 10 acres were $3 a year and when they jumped to $7 he was ready to go to war . . . He is getting used to it and makes no fuss."

Begue gave his impressions on the appearance of the valley *c.* 1910:

> At that time the east end of the valley from the foot of the Verdugo Hills to the foot of the mountains east of Haines canyon was covered with large live oak trees. The oak trees grew to a line on the northwest nearly corresponding to the line of the present Haines canyon flood control channel, and extended all down the valley south of Foothill boulevard To Sunland park.

The article finishes Begue's thought:

> Above the line of the oak trees the present Tujunga town site was covered with a thick cover of greasewood, wild cherry and other shrubs. Bears used to come down from the mountains in the fall, Mr. Begue says, and eat the wild cherries. They seemed to like the film of pulp between the skin and the pit, and also to get some satisfaction out of the pits.
>
>   At the mouth of Haines canyon there was a large grove of Douglas spruce trees, about an acre and a half. Some of the trees were as large as 4 feet in diameter. Spruce trees of similar size grew the whole length of Haines canyon.

The canyons, said Mr. Begue, were named for woodcutters: Haines, Blanchard, Cook, Pickens, Dunsmuir, and all the others along the slope of the Sierra Madre

THE BEGUE BARN. This barn is still standing. The Begues came to Tujunga as bee keepers. As time went by, the family had a successful ranch on which they grew grapes, fruit trees, and gardens.

to Arroyo Seco. Each left his name to the canyon in which he operated. The oaks and spruce were chopped down and cut into 4-foot cord wood, then hauled to Los Angeles to make fires for burning brick.

The thick groves of spruce in the canyons, of course, prevented the damage from heavy deluges of rock, sand, and silt that wash down during rainstorms, especially the storms that come after fires. The settlers dug out or cut down the oaks to make way for vineyards, but did not cut all of the trees to the ground. Some trees sent out new growth. The bee keepers cut brush for their stands or set fire to it. Woodcutters cut the large trees.

Begue said that the south slope of Mount Gleason was covered with big manzanita bushes and yellow pines. "Then came the big fire that swept the whole range as clean as a cement pavement."

The Fehlhaber family ranch lay adjacent to the Begue ranch. The Fehlhabers had cleared the land and planted 45 acres of grapes. The year 1906 was full of promise. The old house, maybe the oldest in Tujunga, built in 1895, was small but solid. Water was available from a deep spring behind the house. There was a grove of native California Oaks along the west side. The five children began watering all their new plants by hand. They soon planted peach and other fruit trees, raised pigs, chickens, and a few horses. There were plenty of deer.

The grapes they produced were rich in tartar, a necessary ingredient in the making of munitions, an industry fed by the growing war of 1914. The family

FEHLHABER HOME. This house, said to be the oldest in Tujunga, was built in 1895.

prospered. When the war ended, the need for munitions decreased. Prohibition was law and wine was not, so grapes were difficult to sell. Once, Ray Fehlhaber delivered 60 lugs of choice grapes to a wholesaler in nearby Montrose and came home with just $5. The family did not give up; they just made some changes.

The Fehlhabers converted their Cadillac into a make-shift truck. They leased some land to a mining company. Part of the riverbed that ran unchanneled through the ranch was turned into a shooting range used by the police and the public. "Ma" Fehlhaber collected the money for its use and gathered up brass cartridges for cash redemption. A roadside fruit stand was built and became a landmark on the Horsethief Trail.

The grove of oak trees was used to allow passing families picnic space for 50¢ and was also used for large organizational get-togethers. As time went by, the fee included barbecues presented by the family. Several grated fireplaces for grilling were provided and a cement slab was added for dances and badminton. Fehlhaber's place grew to become the most popular place in town. A picnic at Oak Grove was special. The brothers did the barbecuing, all night long tending the fire heated by rock in the bottom of the pits. The Fehlhabers exemplified the pioneer spirit in their willingness to adjust to change, persevere, and succeed in all they did.

Other names of early settlers are remembered: John Cox, who was probably the first person to live on the land in Tujunga, the Petrotta family, and the Ardizzones to name a few. All of them paved the way for the community of Tujunga today.

A scrapbook was found, due to some digging around in a dusty, dark closet, containing information about a strong and vital group which formed the community of Sunland-Tujunga, American Legion Post #250. There have been many service clubs, women's groups, church, and community groups which contributed to the growth and welfare of the community and its inhabitants. The Legion group is a good example of this selfless volunteering in any town. Quotations from the scrapbook illustrate activities:

> After working amongst the ex-service men in the Tujunga Valley for a period of about nine months, Joseph W. Forster finally succeeded, with the assistance of Wm. H. Gale, in assembling for their first meeting, twelve ex-service men at Bolton Hall in Tujunga, on January 6th, 1921, at which time the organization of Monte Vista Post #250 was accomplished, and the names of fifteen ex-service men were affixed to an application for a Post Charter of the American Legion.

With the attitudes of pride and promotion, the Legion first organized the Moon Festival, which, they say, gave wonderful publicity and led to a rise in population of the town.

The accomplishments of the Legion are far too numerous to mention. From a short perusal of the scrapbook, it was found that there was a list of 45 major community-changing accomplishments by the Legion just through the year 1935, the last entry in the book.

In December 1921, the first Rifle Association was formed by Monte Vista Post. The first Boy Scout troop in the valley was organized under the leadership of Comrade Maxwell Hill. May 1922 marks the first observance of Mother's Day when all members appeared in uniform for the occasion. In June, the first

A FRUIT STAND. This stand, on Tujunga Canyon Boulevard, the road once known as "Horsethief Trail," was operated by the Fehlhaber family.

barbecue was held at the Begue ranch and in December, the first of the annual turkey shoots at the Begue's was held ("Legion Nets $40 at Turkey Shoot"). In order to carry on the financial responsibilities of the organization, dances, plays, and performances were arranged.

"At a post meeting of August 2nd, 1923, Doctor Theobald gave the news to the post of the death of President Harding. Immediately arrangements were made for the proper observance of the sad occasion." November 11, 1923 was the inauguration for the Annual Observance of Armistice Day.

February 13, 1924 marked the dedication of the hall for the Legion, whose membership had purchased the old clubhouse, and the name Bolton Hall became Legion Hall. "The auxiliary, ever willing to render assistance to the post this year presented us with the beautiful Silk Colors so proudly displayed by our organization."

The membership in 1921 was 43 members; in 1930 it had grown to 105. The group served the community in many ways, such as school programs for patriotism and Americanism; creation of an addendum to the McGroarty *Mission Play*; honoring of veterans; collecting relics from battlefields; and entrance into political matters (including cheaper water rates, pedestrian crossing signs, and a bond issue for veterans).

One member formed a boys' band; later a drum and bugle corps was started. The group held fireworks shows, memorial services, a fall festival (much like the street fair), elected a festival queen, held poppy dances and drives, sponsored a baseball team, gave medals to scholars, and more.

As sponsors of food drives and Christmas baskets, they hit a wall one year. There were so many needy families in 1932 that the group was overwhelmed.

AMERICAN LEGION HALL. American Legion Post #250 was a vital organization that did many selfless voluntary acts for the town. The hall was built in 1924.

They could not fill the orders for the 300 baskets needed, so they held a dinner on December 24 in the basement of the (present) Legion Hall for those 300 families, some families having 12 members.

One can see the vitality, idealism, and importance of this group. In November 1929, the City of Tujunga purchased Bolton Hall, once the Little Landers clubhouse, to be used as the Tujunga town hall with money from a bond issue. The sum of $12,000 went to the Tujunga Post and $3,000 allowed for repairs and alterations. The name again became Bolton Hall. By 1930, the group's name was changed to Tujunga Post #250.

The Legion then began plans for the building of its own hall. They expected to spend about $6,000 on the building and $1,000 on equipment, planned for a Spanish style, about 40 feet by 70 feet with a recreation hall in the basement. This hall, on Pinewood, is still in use by its members today.

Transportation was a crucial element to Tujunga's development. When you remember the children getting to school with pony carts and farmers working with horses and donkeys, it is easy to appreciate the horseless carriage. In about the year 1910, two faithful old mules pulled the lumber-loaded wagons from Glendale for the building of the first homes in the new Tujunga subdivision. The Rowleys hauled out cut wood to the city on "sleds" from the hills to where they could transfer the wood to a wagon.

It was important for the real estate people to get customers from the trains into the valley, so many conveyances were tried. The Rowleys had a two-seated surrey to bring passengers of hunting parties back and forth from the Roscoe station. The people would be treated to barbeques and big beer busts and allowed to view their Tujunga land at a distance from the Monte Vista Hotel. In 1912, the people looking for land were brought in from Los Angeles by train to Roscoe and then by tallyho from Roscoe to Sunland. (A tallyho was a grandiose stage coach that would carry quite a load of people visiting for the weekend.)

Chan Livingston wrote that to get supplies, "it was an all-day trek by horse cart to either Glendale or San Fernando for a fresh supply of groceries and we made that every two weeks."

The Rowleys created the first freight line, first a horse and wagon, then one truck, which they purchased to haul produce of grapes, oranges, and lemons from the valley into Sunland. When the truck broke down, they would haul it (the truck) by horse 10 miles to Burbank to have it repaired.

For social events, most people rode mules or horses if they chose not to walk or used some horse-drawn conveyance. It must have been quite a sight to see the bobbing lantern lights on a Saturday night as people walked up the hilly streets to the dance at Bolton Hall.

As early as 1910, Marshal Hartranft had the two-cylinder Buick pick-up truck with no top and seats along the sides. That was the first auto stage. Later, Earl Simms bought a Cadillac and started a stage line to Glendale's Pacific Electric Station at Brand and Broadway.

ONE OF THE FIRST AUTO STAGES, C. 1910. It was important to bring customers from the railroad to town in as comfortable a manner as possible.

Students were transported in the early days from the Glorietta School in Tujunga to Glendale High School. Chan Livingston wrote that Ed Thoms and Earl Simms, owner-operators of the bus system when Chan went to Glendale High School, discarded their old Buick with the box body to buy two Cadillac buses, 1908 and 1909 models. With the two Cadillacs and their soft seats and tops, "we boys believed we were flirting with the rich. The full-fare passengers, including girl students, had the seat priority; we boys had to hang on like monkeys. Those old Cads had running boards and we rode sitting on the front or rear fenders." Some families moved nearer to the school. The boys could stand the 10-mile cart ride, but the girls could not.

After being bought, divided, sold, and added to, the company called the Los Angeles-Glendale-Montrose-Sunland-via La Crescenta-Highway Highlands-Tujunga Motor Coach Line (LAGMSLCHHT Motor Coach Line) had built up to 27 round-trips daily by 1932. The run from Sunland to Los Angeles took 70 minutes; the trip is 20 minutes on the freeway today. The public transportation system, serving Verdugo Valley commuters, was started by the Verdugo Hills Transportation Company in 1918. Company founder Al Richardson offered a 2-hour service with 14-passenger Studebakers to service Tujunga's population of around 1,000 and Sunland's smaller population of 200.

On the first paved street, Foothill Boulevard (once called Michigan Avenue), Model Ts strained every bearing to head up the hill from Sunland to the top of Tujunga from a dead start. If the clutch slipped, it meant aching calves the next morning.

There was much written about those newfangled contraptions, the Tin Lizzies. By the end of the 1920s, the homely Tin Lizzie had indeed blossomed into the universal car. Nearly 4 million of them, all nearly alike as Ford had said they should be, were rattling around the country. By providing more or less instant transportation for the mass of American people, they were transforming a horse-and-buggy land of isolated villages into a mobile, modern nation.

The following was recorded by the Little Landers Historical Society:

> By 1910 it cost less to drive a Maxwell automobile than a horse and buggy—1.8 cents per passenger mile as against 2.5 cents for horse and buggy. By 1924, a new Ford cost no more than a good buggy horse. . . You could pick out any color you wanted as long as it was black.

One could pay $350 in Tujunga at Anderson's (the first local Ford dealer) for a brand new Model T in that year. Hercules gas fueled the autos. The first gas station in Los Angeles opened in 1912.

Henry Ford once said, "The jokes about my car sure helped to popularize it." For a good part of the decade, the flood of Ford jokes seemed unstoppable. In the daily commentary, they were as much a part of conversation as politics or the weather. Vaudeville monologists could get a guaranteed laugh by taunting the T; doctors cheered up their patients with quips about the flivver. The jibes were compiled in paperback booklets; the hawker cried, "Peanuts, oranges, candy, cigars, and Ford joke books, two hundred jokes for only 15¢," at train stations. A

EVERYONE WAS ON WHEELS. The horse cart and wagon stayed at home while the folks from downtown took a Sunday drive to their favorite entertainment area.

man on his deathbed had a final request—that his flivver be buried with him because "he had never been in a hole yet where his Ford car couldn't get him out."

It had been part of the dream, and part of the sales pitch, that the Pacific Electric street car line was to come to Sunland-Tujunga. At the beginning of the Tujunga land sales in 1910, Hartranft drove his two-cylinder Buick pickup truck, which was much more comfortable than the horse-and-buggy-stage before it, but still made a hot, dusty sideways ride all the way from the city. So, after a day of work, it would have been a lot better to ride from Los Angeles clear on to Sunland on the Pacific Electric Railway.

When Earl Sims bought his Cadillac and started a stage line to the Glendale Pacific Electric Station at Brand and Broadway, the ride was a bit easier, but long. There was a jitney provided later on, which was an open air affair. The jitney ran on Verdugo Road from Glendale as far as Pennsylvania and Foothill in La Crescenta, about two miles from the boundary of Tujunga. It was supposed to have continued up to Tujunga Canyon Boulevard, but that just did not happen.

There were advertisements that street car service was to be extended to Stonehurst to the west in Sun Valley, and from Burbank in the other direction. The story was written up in the *Herald Examiner*—neither line was provided. Hopes and promises had been around for a long time: "rail line coming!" In 1916, citizens discussed the rail line, even as far as being canvassed to see who would donate right-of-way and pay a bonus in dollars.

In 1920, two transportation issues made the folks talk about the need for rail service in the Tujunga Valley: the Glendale-Glorietta and Sunland stage tipping

JITNEY BUS. Any transportation was better than the horse and buggy. This "bus" offered a faster, less dusty ride to the Red Line in Glendale.

over and the Pacific Electric cars taking passengers comfortably from Los Angeles to San Gabriel.

The Glendale-Glorietta and Sunland stage once tipped en route from Sunland to Los Angeles. Ten passengers suffered bruises and cuts and one passenger died. At the same time, play-goers going to see J.S. McGroarty's *Mission Play* rode in comfort from Los Angeles to San Gabriel via Pacific Electric cars. The desire for transportation to the foothills was rekindled in the minds of Sunland-Tujunga dwellers as they saw other communities succeed in adding electric rail or Pacific Electric bus service. In 1936, the local residents were invited to a hearing. An application for bus service from Tujunga to North Hollywood was made to the Railroad Commission. That helped.

The Pacific Electric car, a narrow gauge inter-urban network, was first a horse trolley in Los Angeles. The beginning of the electric car came shortly after. In 1895, a line ran from downtown Los Angeles to Pasadena. By 1902, a standard gauge car was running, the line having been purchased by Henry Huntington. By the time the Little Landers Colony in Tujunga was beginning in 1913, electric cars from Long Beach were going all over southern California. The cars were wooden, then later built with steel for increased safety.

It has been said that Sunland and Tujunga have always had "dinky" service. A Pacific Electric street car line used to connect the La Crescenta-Montrose area with Glendale. The trolley ran up what is now Canada Boulevard, crossing the road at the La Crescenta-Verdugo intersection. It followed the parkway to the Montrose business district, then followed Montrose Avenue to end at Pennsylvania Avenue. A right-of-way to Marcus street in Tujunga was provided, but the rail was never built. The dinky ride was fine, but the walk downhill to Sunland was a long one.

During peak hours, the Pacific Electric sent larger cars over that route, but for the most part, the cars were still of the dinky variety, meaning "short." This Toonerville–type car pitched and tossed like a boat at sea as it careened down the uneven roadbed. Old-timers said that the trip to Glendale was breathtaking and swift. Meanwhile, the trolley never got to Sunland-Tujunga and never will.

85

8. To Build a City

Growth of the settlements of Monte Vista and the Little Lands Colony eventually resulted in the merging of the two communities into essentially one town, though they remain separate by name.

Sunland grew quietly as an agricultural community with a small business area. The prime land was in the low part of the valley. Tujunga leaders wanted to annex Sunland, but Sunland's residents fought the proposition. After a time of upheaval, Sunland had not been able to agree on whether to annex to the City of Los Angeles, incorporate with Tujunga, or just forget the whole thing. The decision was made, after much controversy, to annex to Los Angeles in 1926.

There were three main stages in the growth of the town of Tujunga, separate from that of Sunland: the first began when the Hartranft's Western Empire Lands were first subdivided; the second was when the town site opened in 1913; and the third began at the close of the Great World War. It was then, as early as 1914, when the country saw an economic recession. The colony had been struggling to maintain existence, then the war came, drawing the young colonists away who went to serve their country. Many left because their small holdings were too small for economic profit, while others became disenchanted with the "ideal life" and moved on to more lucrative ventures. By 1915, town meeting government had ceased to operate. By 1920, the Little Landers colony was no longer viable. By April 21, 1925, the people had formed the city of Tujunga, a city of the sixth class, with John Russell as the first mayor.

Earlier resistance to change happened when Tujunga wanted Sunland to annex to it. Words were written in songs, such as those in the booklet *Ballads of Annexation* or *Songs That Went With Victory*, written by Ralph Seaton Irish in 1926. In the preface of the book it says, "These little campaign songs were written to strengthen our contention and further our cause in the battle we are waging for justice." The subject of the contention was the threatened "forced" annexation of Sunland to Tujunga, which then led to the annexation of Sunland to Los Angeles in 1926.

Sunland found that when they approached the county supervisors about incorporating as a city of the sixth class, the action would not exclude them from paying taxes for the Sunland-Tujunga fire district, although they would own their own fire department. The county denied their petition to incorporate, the reason being that there would be a possible water shortage.

According to Ralph Irish, "Tujungans used to look down on the green fertile valley of Sunland, with its beautiful orchards and vineyards, and its magnificent oak park, with eager and covetous eyes, until their desire to their own little municipality became an obsession."

Sunland people voted down annexation in the 1925 election, but the Tujungans were not satisfied with the rebuke. Irish states, "through gerrymandering, and manipulation, and scheming they were able to annex about four square miles of territory to their little city, at an election where only 8 votes were cast."

The location of that territory, says Irish, prevented Sunland from becoming a part of Glendale or Burbank, which were just beyond the Verdugo Hills to the south of Sunland. Sunland people woke up to the realization that Tujungans planned to annex Sunland territory bit by bit, so the majority of citizens decided to annex to Los Angeles. They thought that they would receive more and greater benefits with a smaller amount of taxation by going to a larger, more organized city. Better benefits, some thought, than "we would have from a small city of the

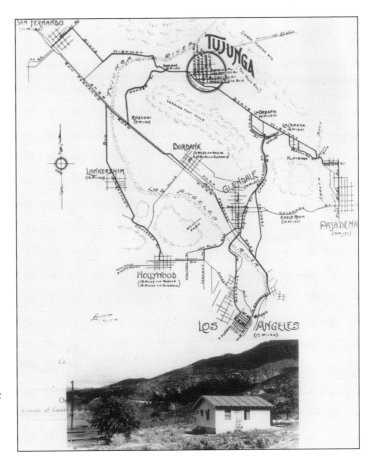

ADVERTISING MAP. This advertising map shows the location of Sunland-Tujunga in relation to Los Angeles and the other major cities. It was probably printed in the 1920s.

sixth class, which is bonded to the limit, and where petty politics and bossism is always in evidence. . . ."

In an earlier election and amid controversy, 539 votes were cast: 328 for annexation of Sunland to Los Angeles, 211 against. Tujunga attempted a coup. Irish recounts the dispute:

> The line of territory they proposed to annex was so gerrymandered as to include all the vacant lots and lands they could connect in Sunland, carefully manipulated so as to leave out all the homes of voters opposed to their annexation, thus converting Sunland into a group of islands, so to speak, with no outlet except across a strip of Tujunga territory; taking from one pioneer over 80 years old about one hundred acres of vineyards and orchards which he had spent almost a half century in beautifying and perfecting, and then had the bad grace and dishonesty to leave his residence with a small tract of land out to keep him from voting against them, thus disenfranchising him . . . They also included in this annexation strip, Sunland's Big Oak Park, widely known as Monte Vista Park.

This coup was in the form of an election held 30 days before the general election to annex to Los Angeles. Irish wrote, "Six hundred voters were disenfranchised from voting, only 22 voters taking part in the election. They took the property of many voters, left their residence out so there would be no opposition to their scheme."

HARRY ZACHAU AND HIS WIFE. *Shown here at their home, the Zachaus kept a healthy farm on 72 barren hillside acres.*

There were 16 booster songs, all written by Ralph Irish, with words like: "There's a just cause for vexation, which has charged the very air, and bombs of annexation are bursting everywhere. Work together as a whole—with Tujunga for the doughnut, and Sunland for the [hole] . . . when any plums are offered, they'll put it to a vote, and Tujunga'll get the pudding, and Sunland be the goat."

A resident of Tujunga since 1910, Harry W. Zachau was a hardy pioneer who helped develop Tujunga into a thriving town through careful use of his property, as well as his civic and organizational activities. A news article tells about Zachau's passage, and what he had to give up, as he experienced change in a growing community:

> beloved acres to County Flood Control—The price of progress is often hard to pay. This truth has been etched sharply on the minds of Mr. and Mrs. Zachau, pioneer Tujunga homesteaders, on whose beloved hillside acres the Los Angeles Flood Control District has gouged out a vast debris basin in Zachau Canyon which lies north and east of Tujunga Canyon Boulevard.
>
> Not that the debris basin wasn't needed—it was. Because each winter—some worse than others—rain from an eight-square-mile watershed in the San Gabriel mountains would wash in torrents down Zachau Canyon, sweeping debris before it and inundating wide residential districts along Wentworth Street.
>
> The county was commissioned to control those flood waters and it has.
>
> With an even larger installation in Rowley Canyon to the south completed in 1955, the County has slowed to a trickle any flood waters that rampage out of the hills, funneling them into the recently installed storm drains of Hillrose and Wentworth.
>
> But such progress is costly in money and emotions, and somebody usually gets hurt.

In 1910, Harry Zachau and his wife had settled on 72 acres of barren hillside overlooking a deep, tree-lined canyon to which Zachau gave his name. For over 46 years, springs in the canyon supplied the water needed to grow the citrus and other fruit trees, as well as pines, maples, and other shade trees.

For years, the family cultivated several acres of alfalfa for their livestock and always kept a garden of fresh vegetables. The reporter continues his description with the following:

> But the County, on a mandate from the people, sent in their giant earth movers and swept the canyon clean of oaks and tall sycamores. It scraped and gouged the canyon floor, condemned and cut through a huge hill, built a dam and a concrete spillway and a half-mile long concrete channel from the spillway down to Tujunga Canyon Boulevard and connected it with the Wentworth storm drain.

Now, day and night down this impervious cement channel flows Zachau's precious spring water, wasted and lost on its way to Big Tujunga Wash.

The Zachaus have had to request service from the city's Bureau of Water and Power to bring water to all that is left of their original homestead. The County, of course, paid the Zachaus for the property.

The debris basin cost $202,700 to build. It covers about one-third of a square mile. Work started in August of 1955 to remove approximately 108,000 cubic yards of earth and line the channel with concrete. At peak periods, 40 men were employed.

The deepest section is 19 feet deep and held a maximum of 38,000 cubic yards of water and debris. The basin was one of many flood channel projects designed to contain the torrents of water that rush into the valleys during the infrequent but powerful floods.

The trustees also had to draw up ordinances. The first ruling was that a copy of all ordinances were to be posted in three places: the Legion Hall (Bolton), the Tujunga Valley Bank, and the Tujunga Drug Company. These ordinances were for "the immediate preservation of the public peace, health and safety of the people of Tujunga."

The day that Tujunga became an incorporated city—April 21, 1925—a board of trustees was elected. Its first action was to draw up ordinances. The first ruling was that a copy of all ordinances was to be posted in three places: the Legion Hall (in Bolton Hall), the Tujunga Valley Bank, and the Tujunga Drug Co. These ordinances were for "the immediate preservation of the public peace, health and safety of the people of Tujunga."

Ordinances for compensations amounted to $25 per month for the clerk, $150 for the marshal, and $1 for the treasurer. Commissioners were appointed: commissioners of streets, sidewalks, and parks, of health and safety, of city planning and zoning, and of fire and police. The president of the board was the Commissioner of Finance.

Punishment was fixed for any board member, or any person, for using profane, vulgar, loud, or boisterous language, for interrupting the proceedings, for refusing to be seated, or for members who neglected attendance at meetings. The fine would not exceed $25, imprisonment not exceeding 10 days.

License fees were set for businesses: dance halls cost $30 per quarter, billiard halls $4, traveling circuses $5 per day. Lumber yards paid $6 a quarter, as did drug stores and sanitariums. The penalty was a fine of not more than $100 and imprisonment of not more than 50 days in the city jail.

After a couple of years, a new law was fixed: there was to be no spitting on the sidewalk. When the city was first incorporated and the trustees were adopting the health ordinance, this inhibition was left out, since Tujunga had no sidewalks to spit on. It was thought that the rocks and dirt were the safest and most sanitary place for public cuspidors.

HARRY ZACHAU'S FAMILY STORE. Zachau owned and operated a general merchandise store in Tujunga.

Germs were a problem. Many of the rules had to do with communicable diseases. Quarantine rules and disinfection rules for the public, doctors, and undertakers were strictly spelled out.

Ordinance 19, section 16, states that no milkman shall take away bottles or receptacles from any place in which people were ill with contagious disease. This included "scarlet fever, cholera, typhus, diphtheria, plague, membranous croup, leprosy, anthrax, meningitis, whooping cough, typhoid fever, dysentery, trachoma or tetanus." It was unlawful for such milkmen, dealers, or distributors to consider any further sales until the health department investigated.

The subjects of cesspools, sewage, and privies were addressed. Even in 1925, no privy or water closet was to be operated without a water-flushed toilet.

There were rules about the transporting of steam shovels over city streets, about obstructing streets, and of "moving" city property. Two blasts of the policeman's whistle meant that one must stop. There was to be no driving on sidewalks. Vehicles traveling after sunset had to have a lamp on the left side of the vehicle. Dogs that attacked and bit a person were to be killed by their owners. Druggists were not to dispense intoxicating medicines. Guns were not allowed to be fired. There were severe restrictions on fireworks. It was stated that "vehicles may be parked on both sides of Michigan Avenue [now Foothill Boulevard] at an angle of forty-five degrees between Fischer [current name not known] and Sunset [now Commerce Avenue]."

One would not want to place any bets on any game not mentioned in section 330 or he could be fined $500 and could spend 6 months in the Tujunga jail. The announcement was made that "We all must be sure to check on the latest ordinances posted at the legion hall, the Tujunga Valley Bank or the Tujunga Drug Company."

Jail cells were also one of the first items of business. It was costing $1 a day to keep a prisoner in the downtown county jail. For a token $1, two iron cells were purchased from the city of Glendale and added to the back of the Bolton Hall building. That was 1926, the same year a fire station was built.

Several elections were held before Tujunga was voted to become an incorporated city—811 votes were cast in the final election, with 457 for incorporation and 354 against. The seal for the new city was a circular disk, 1.875 inches in diameter, with "City of Tujunga California, incorporated May 1, 1925" inscribed on it. The official flower was the zinnia.

The first trustees meeting was held in June to set salaries, select officials, and begin business. Serving were Misters Russell, Zachau, Myers, Miller, and Bodkin. Bertha Morgan was city clerk and A. Adams was treasurer. Harry Zachau was one of the first trustees.

When the citizens of Tujunga considered annexation to the city of Los Angeles, the outcry was considerably louder than that of the Sunland folks had been. It was in 1926, just a year after the town of Tujunga had voted to become an incorporated city of the sixth class, that the citizens began to talk of annexing to Los Angeles. Within a year, the campaign really got rolling. There was still a considerable number of voters against annexation. Each year, there was another vote until, in 1932, the city of Tujunga became part of the city of Los Angeles.

Sometimes, when there are two sides to an issue, there can be negotiation and compromise. In 1932, though, there did not seem to be any middle ground. Mabel Hatch summed up the facts of a Tujunga feud, that of the question of whether or not the city of Tujunga would annex to the city of Los Angeles:

> The question of annexation to the City of Los Angeles was one of the most controversial which ever plagued and divided the people of the Verdugo Valley. The residents . . . were deeply conscious of its importance, and they fought with all they had, some on one side and some on the other, for what they thought were the best interests of their town. They knew the long shadow of that decision would lay across the valley for many a year.
>
> The heart of the discussion was water. Annexationists felt all services would be improved under the protecting wing of a big city with its vast resources . . .

Those included the protection of a consistent water supply. Unless Tujunga annexed to the city, some said, the town would be left high and dry with no water at all. The anti-annexationists, on the other hand, were sure the town had adequate supplies of water and electricity.

In June of 1927, the Tujunga campaign really got rolling. In spite of the conflict, the small city forged ahead with all the established departments working exceptionally well. The fire chief, Harry Rice, was doing a splendid job of fire fighting. The police chiefs, Earl Brunner and Ray Elkin, had done fine work and there were no felonies during the year of 1927. There were 167 building permits that year.

After voting about the question of annexation in 1927 (354 for and 594 against), again in 1930 (585 for to 430 against), and once more in 1931, the agitation still continued. Annexation won by a vote of 718 ayes to 659 nays on January 5, 1932, a simple majority of 59 votes. In March of that year, officials of Los Angeles were given the keys to Tujunga City Hall.

A peculiar thing had happened about the time between the third and fourth elections for annexation. Suddenly, after the third, every house, shack, and building in Tujunga became occupied. The newcomers registered and became voters. Then, the morning after the annexation was established, there was a great exodus and plenty of empty houses appeared once again. The election was protested in the courts, but nothing was accomplished, and Tujunga became for all time a part of Los Angeles.

One resident, then a young girl of the Forster family, said recently that after the results were known that annexation was established, the family rushed home, turned off all the lights, and hid. They were on the side of the anti-annexation and they were afraid. According to Postmaster Tom Theobald, street names were changed right away. Even the anti- annexation groups who had streets named for their families, watched as those names were changed by the city.

THE HOME OF THE FORSTER FAMILY. In the living room of this house, the Lady of Lourdes Catholic Church was started. When annexation was established, the entire family hid here in fear.

TOM THEOBOLD. The Tujunga postmaster spoke of the bitter fight over annexation when neighbors wouldn't talk to each other.

One of the first effects of annexation was on real estate taxes. On January 1, 1930, the tax rate for the City of Tujunga was $3.57; of Los Angeles $4.25. The Tujunga rate was naturally raised at once to the Los Angeles rate as soon as it became a part of the city. In joining the larger city, Tujunga automatically assumed its share of the millions of dollars of bonded indebtedness of the city. (Los Angeles refused to assume any part of the debt of $700 on Tujunga City Hall and the residents had to pay that off by a 10¢ increase in the tax rate).

One does wonder if water was the only issue involved in annexation. The *Record Ledger* headlines from 1927 read: "Tujunga Remains Calm In Foreshadow Of Oil Boom" and "Well Going Down In Tujunga Wash; Joseph Hummel, Operator, Says He Is Confident His 200-Acre Lease Covers Great Oil Pool—Expects Sand At 800 Ft."

The valley had yielded some gold, silver, silica, graphite, tin, and copper from mines worked over the few years. As a natural resource, water was the most precious. In 1927, and even earlier, the experts believed they would find rich oil deposits.

The report continues, "most of the oil excitement in the Verdugo Hills is centered in La Crescenta and Verdugo City, but the only actual drilling is in the Big Tujunga wash at the lower end of the Tujunga Valley just west of the Sunland cannery." One outfit with a portable rig went down to 120 feet, changed to rotary tools, and waited for the great pool of oil to be forced out by the strong below-ground gas pressure.

At first, the shaft was dug by hand to 36 feet, where they hit water. They then went down with a drill to 115 feet, "at which point they believed they were through the boulders in formation that can be handled with a rotary to advantage." Four lines of cable were used to hoist the boulders, the "huge fellows." Hummel would go down 800 feet and if that was not deep enough, he would sink a shaft to strike second sand at 1,700 feet. He was pretty sure of the promise of oil because he had been right in his geological calculations 100 percent of his 39 tries.

Old-timers had reported oil shale and seepage in several areas, including Haines Canyon. Leo Lang said he recalled running his plow into a heavy seepage on the Paul Heffleman ranch. He said that he had "run that plow into the sticky mess one day and a team of frisky horses yanked the beam out of his plow." The old timers were apathetic about the project, since they believed the amount of oil to be small.

The people in the Crescenta Valley and Verdugo City withdrew their lands from sale and crowds gathered for meetings. The real estate boom was dwarfed by the frenzied speculation for oil and many wells were dug. Leases were obtained in Sunland and Tujunga from a number of local residents with a clause that a test well had to be dug within 90 days. Later, in 1939, the shale found in Lopez Canyon showed great promise.

But there was no pool of oil. The first reference in the records was found as early as 1920, the last reference in 1939. When the 210 Freeway was roughed out, oil shale and seepage was seen there, but there was no mention of drilling.

The gold played out, no one mentions silver or silica or any of the others. There is still a substantial watershed in the Big Tujunga Canyon, which always acts as a very important part of the water supply of Los Angeles. There is also a thriving rock and gravel industry which is now operating downstream in Sun Valley.

9. Commerce and Culture

Mail service, or long distance communication, seems to be one of the first developments of any civilization. In the early years of the United States, the overland stage express, pony express, and the railroad carried mail across the country. In 1860, mail delivery took ten days from Missouri to Sacramento; in 1900, it took two days by rail; and by 1950, air delivery made it a day and a half.

Perhaps the story of Daisy Bell Rinehart's buckboard, which brought the mail to Sunland in 1885, is not one of history's great moments, but Rinehart was quite important to the people in the Sunland Valley. She picked up the Sunland mail at Roscoe (Sun Valley), about 6-8 miles away, from the steam trains. The train depots were called "flag stops" because passengers signaled the train when they wanted to board. Rinehart drove her pony and buckboard into Roscoe over what is now Sunland Boulevard, but was at that time a rugged and narrow dirt road. After each rain, the first team over the road would make a new trail, bypassing deep chuckholes and the courses the new rivers had made, while jackrabbits galloped across the road in front of the buckboard.

There is a report in a 1959 copy of the *Record Ledger* of a time during the early days of the rural delivery that "a runaway horse scattered the mail over the countryside. That day the mail literally blew into town. Those who saw it declared as how this was the first air mail service."

The first post office at Monte Vista was established on April 2, 1887. It was to be located "one mile East of Tujunga River and four miles East of the Southern Pacific Railroad tracks." In the earliest days of the settlement, a post office was located in a building on Fenwick Street. Postmasters serving from 1887 to 1900 were Wesley True Moulton, Loren T. Rowley, Virginia Rowley, and Henry C. Bowers.

Whatever constituted a post office was later moved to the home of Mrs. George Huse, who served as postmaster, then later into the general store located near Sunland Park, where the grocer handled both mail and sales. Soon after, it was moved across the street to the "Sweet Shop" of Fred Herron. During the year 1916, the average daily receipts were 50¢.

In 1936, under the direction of Madge Kearns, mail delivery was serving 198 families. By 1939, the growth of the town could be measured by the increase in

POSTMASTER. Before 1920, the mail was delivered from the steam train in Roscoe to the highway in Tujunga at Commerce Avenue (then called Sunset Avenue), and wheeled up the hill to the post office in a wheelbarrow.

post office box rentals, which rose to 400. In 1940, the post office was established on Foothill Boulevard. Floor space of 1,320 feet and 570 lock boxes were needed. It is amusing that, in 1967, the new post office was opened on Fenwick and Sherman Grove, almost where it began. Madge Kearns, postmistress in 1954, reportedly got a big kick out of the new red, white, and blue mail delivery trucks—the ones with the right hand drive (built for easy delivery). Sunland Post Office was the first in Los Angeles County to receive them.

The Tujunga "Little Lands" post office had opened in 1914 on the corner of present-day Commerce Avenue and Valmont. Moving from corner to corner, it occupied that location for 52 years. The first postmaster, Frederick Mason Ashby, also served as moderator of town meetings of the Little Lands Colony.

There was a time when Commerce Avenue, the main thoroughfare in Tujunga, was full of shoppers. There was plenty of chaparral on the street in the empty lots. At first, the avenue was a wide, unpaved road without sidewalks or curbs. The only store available was the cooperative store for the Little Landers Colony. Soon, other businesses opened. Dean's Dry Goods was one of the first, where everything from mouse traps to calico was sold. If Charles Dean didn't have something, he'd go down to Los Angeles to get it. The first honest-to-goodness barber shop in the valley was in the back part of Dean's store.

COMMERCE AVENUE, 1925. Commerce Avenue, the main street of Tujunga, was once a bustling business community.

Later, there were other businesses such as Herron's Sweet Shop, G.B. Patterson's meat market, Tujunga Drug with Arthur Stover as pharmacist, McLean's Drug Store, and Guiseppe Logreco's bakery.

As time went by, the Tujunga post office was located at Sunset and El Centro. A library had been established and the Farmers and Merchants bank was built. The Jewel Theater opened up. Sodas and candy for the kids were for sale at the drug store, as well as medicine, sundries, and tobacco. There was also a Chinese laundry.

Advertisements in the *Record Ledger* show that the town had several doctors, dentists, and sanatoriums. From 1913 through probably the 1950s, the town had every product and service anyone would need. During the 1920s, Verdugo Hills Realty was selling roomy lots for $10 a month. The grocery store was selling cans of corn and peas for 15¢ a can, catsup by the pint at 17¢.

From the chamber of commerce edition of the *Sentinel Magazine* dated May 25, 1922, we can see more clearly what the main street of Commerce Avenue was like. On a walk from Highway, going uphill, one would pass the Californian Home Extension Real Estate office on the corner with the Verdugo Hills Transportation Company across the street. Walking up Sunset, we'd come to The Fair Dry Goods, Wright's Shoe store, Canaday's Electrical Supplies, Tujunga Paint and Paper, Dean's Dry Goods, Ashby's Drug and Stationary (and Post Office), and Bolton Hall Community Center.

Down the hill on the other side of the avenue would be Garman and Sons grocery, G. Buck Real Estate, Insley's Confection, Haines Canyon Water Supply Company, Greer's Barber Shop, Tujunga Valley Bank, the *Record Ledger* newspaper, Caldwell's Feed and Fuel, The Blue Bird restaurant, the *Sentinel Magazine*, and the Sunshine Bake Shop. Close to Commerce Avenue, on the side streets, were the Lumber Company and Tujunga Drug and Jewelry.

The *Sentinel Magazine* from 1922 lists in a roster that on or near to Sunset and El Centro (Commerce and Valmont) were 13 real estate offices, 4 meat markets, 8 places to buy building materials, 2 drug stores, a bank, a post office, a library, 3 garages, 2 gas stations, 13 grocery stores, 2 shoe and shoe repair shops, 2 barber shops, 2 newspapers, 4 eating places, 3 dry goods shops, a cleaners and dyers, 2 laundries, the Haines Canyon Water Supply Company, and the transportation company. From 1913 to 1922, a good-sized town had been formed.

A group of men could usually be seen sitting around town. It would be a beautiful California day. Harry Lamson would have joined the group of men gathered around the old Tujunga Post Office at Valmont and Commerce in Tujunga. As was his habit, he set up his camera. The year would have been 1918. The group gathered was called the Millionaires Club of Happiness and Contentment. Lamson took a few photos of the men that day and preserved a part of Tujunga's history. This group was made famous all over southern California in John Steven McGroarty's pages in the *Los Angeles Times Sunday Magazine*.

This small group of pioneer men gathered around the post office to wait for the mail to be distributed. Wallace Morgan, writing for the *Record Ledger* on May 21, 1953, reported on the group:

> Sometimes there were more, sometimes less, but there was a small core
> of steadies who were on hand almost every day, not because they

AD-MART. *This business is one of the oldest on Commerce Avenue. The Ad-Mart, with a unique idea of the time, was in part of a consignment shop.*

expected more mail so much as because they were too old or too broken in health to work and had time on their hands. Most of these steadies also had seen more prosperous days, and because of the latter fact they adopted the name "Millionaires Club."

The millionaires never had an official membership roll, nor any formal meeting place. They sat on the post office steps, on rocks and boulders that lay where the sidewalk should have been, or squatted on their heels . . . any old time.

As the fame of their club increased, every man in the valley was proud to be a member. In 1921, over 500 people signed the register of the Millionaires Club of Happiness and Contentment, making them members for life.

Morgan goes on to say, "But out of the mainly fictitious Millionaires Club grew a very real and practical influence in the community—a sentiment of good fellowship and noblesse oblige." In the summer months, when dry grass on vacant lots presented a constant fire danger, every millionaire was expected to carry a shovel in his car at all times, ready to throw a shovelful of dirt on a blaze.

When the American Legion needed a meeting place (they wanted to buy Bolton Hall), the Millionaires started a Moon Festival to raise money. During the festival, every millionaire in the Tujunga business district closed his doors and turned out to pull up greasewood and roll boulders.

THE MILLIONAIRES CLUB OF HAPPINESS AND CONTENTMENT. *The club was composed of the men who were "too tired and too sick to work." They spent their time waiting for the mail to be delivered and dreaming of ways to make the town better. They became the first unofficial chamber of commerce.*

"THE MAN WHO PLAYS THE FLUTE." There were names for the members of the Millionaires Club. Another was "The Man Who Played the Radio."

Chan Livingston, when interviewed in 1975, said the following of the club:

> My father was a member of the club. They were men of intense interest applicable to the Sunland-Tujunga area's future. They were the early day wheel horses with the golden rule concept of truth and honesty and were Tujunga's first volunteer city council and chamber of commerce combined.

The photographs of the group show some of the members: Wallace Morgan, who became the owner and publisher of the area's first newspaper, the *Record Ledger*, in 1920; Leo Lang, stone mason and carpenter specializing in early day small dwellings; Marshall Hartranft, land developer and sales promoter; Ashley Hatch, retired federal prison warden; James Livingston; "Doc" Buck; and John Steven McGroarty. Doc Buck was known as "The Man Who Plays the Phonograph." Other members included Harry Lamson, J. Greif, Eli Eby, Ensign Woodruff, Fred Ashby, A.D. Kirshman, Philip Begue, George Harris, Wilmot Parcher, Judge Herman Breidt, and Major Patrick Blake.

Livingston recounts the following in his memoirs:

> my mother instructed me to hitch the horse . . . and drive up the hill and bring your father home . . . he is up there with those other six wind jammers worrying about the troubles and complaints of those Eastern

City Lot Buyers. Tell him to get on home and do some worrying about milking the cow.

He concludes by remembering some overheard words of the 1918 Millionaires, "Gentlemen, one of these days in the future, there will be five hundred families living in these green Verdugo Hills." They all agreed.

One of the men, John Steven McGroarty, who had arrived in Tujunga just before the 1920s, brought the romance of the Green Verdugo Hills and California itself to the attention of the world. McGroarty and his wife Ida built their home in Tujunga in 1923. This home remains as a cultural arts center under the supervision of the Los Angeles Cultural Affairs Department. McGroarty became interested in the history and folklore of California, especially that of the missions.

If one of McGroarty's greatest dreams had been realized, the community would be entirely different today. In February 1923, he made a speech at Bolton Hall to announce plans for the building of the 22nd Franciscan mission. It was to be built somewhere across from Manzanita Park in Tujunga near his home. In his own words: "Some time this summer, if God spares us, we will build this mission and raise another cross to the King of Glory in the Green Verdugo Hills."

The author of the *Record Ledger* article, when reporting on this speech, states that McGroarty's Tujunga neighbors were thrilled with the great inspiration of the wonderful undertaking. In one sense, the construction of the mission would be rated the crowning achievement of McGroarty's life of achievements. The article described the impact of the event:

> For when the Twenty-Second Franciscan Mission is built—the mission of San Juan Evangelista—it will stand in its beautiful setting among the live oak trees, . . . a symbol of reverent faith and devotion, originating in the heart of one man and spreading like the leaven of righteousness to the thousands who have heard him speak as he spoke to the neighbors Monday night.

In his speech, McGroarty had said, "Let other communities do the commonplace things. We will do this great thing." The new mission would be the first built since the historic days of 150 years before when Friar Junipero Serra and his brown-robed priests established the chain of missions reaching from San Diego to San Francisco.

McGroarty added that offers of help were coming in from everywhere. Seymour Thomas of La Crescenta, one of the three greatest portrait painters in the world, had dreamed of a grand painting to be above the altars. Five of Thomas's friends would paint pictures on the walls and ceilings that people would come from all over the world to see. A friend in Glendale told McGroarty to buy the sweetest-toned bell in the world and send him the bill. The War Department had consented to send a battery of artillery from Fort MacArthur to fire a salute when the host was to be raised before the cross on the day of consecration.

"I would like," McGroarty said, "to have Tujunga transformed into a Spanish village for that day." Colonel Ashby, George Buck, and all the other Millionaires were to be in boleros and red sashes, while the women wore beautiful Spanish dresses. "And I want Major Blake and some of the other military men to take charge of handling the crowds, and Phil Begue to look after a great barbecue."

The great cross would be hewn from the trees in the mountains beyond the Tujunga and would be borne on the shoulders of Tujunga Native Americans. There would be a great pageant of Spanish, Native American, and Franciscan representatives across the valley where a trumpeters mass would be held. There would be 100,000 visitors present to witness the event, easily seen from the hillside slopes.

After the speeches of McGroarty and others, music was furnished by members of the Manzanita orchestra. The spirit of the group was high with promise for the future of their fine communities.

However, the 22nd mission was never built. The idea of McGroarty's mission was initiated by a man who had big dreams and a silver tongue. In this case, there were no funds available and the whole idea, sadly, died for lack of continued enthusiasm. If it had been allowed to happen, Sunland, Tujunga, and the surrounding area would be a different place entirely.

A man of many talents, McGroarty was an orator, congressman, columnist, publisher, historian, playwright, poet, and community activist. For 40 years, he worked for the *Los Angeles Times* newspaper and was known for his weekly page

JOHN STEVEN MCGROARTY. Leading citizen J.S. McGroarty was a splendid orator, a columnist for the Los Angeles Times, *author of the world famous* Mission Play, *Poet Laureate of the state of California, and congressman.*

in the magazine section, "The Green Verdugo Hills." Through this publication, he made the Millionaires Club part of the popular culture. He wrote in 1938:

> At the meeting of the Millionaires Club of Contentment and Happiness held at the time of the full moon just past, a subject that is as old as the hills but ever new came up for discussion. The meeting was held on the stone fence from which you can see the sunset on the Ventura Mountains and the lights of the foolish automobiles flitting like fireflies up and down the Calabassas Road.

He then goes on to report that the Millionaires then discussed the subject of the armies of the law: "Armies and vast hordes of the law that were not necessary if every man in the world were the man he ought to be."

These words give a feeling for the kind of romantic and sensitive man McGroarty was. As poet and playwright, he was quite famous. In 1923, the *Mission Players Open Air Drama* was held at the Garden of the Moon on the corner of Foothill and Commerce Avenue. The McGroartys made it possible to see plays that "will be full of high-class music and dancing and brilliant costuming." The proceeds would go to the Legion and to the Episcopal Church.

McGroarty left a legacy in his written word. While traveling in Europe in 1930, he was honored by King Alfonso XIII of Spain. Pope Pius also honored him for his work. He was a well-known poet. After his appointment as Poet Laureate of California, his poem "Just California" was memorized by students all over the state as their first lesson in the story of California.

His famous *Mission Play* was his special love, his own creation. The play depicted the founding of the California missions by Friar Junipero Serra and was, at one time, the top theatrical attraction in southern California—a tourist "must." The play was considered to show authentic scenes based on actual history. Local schools included attendance at the play as a part of their curriculums. Children were bussed to San Gabriel for matinees.

The *Mission Play* was staged over 3,500 times and was seen by more than 2.5 million people from 1912 through 1927. After a 23-week run in 1914, the play took to the road with long and successful shows in San Francisco and San Diego. McGroarty built the San Gabriel Playhouse a few miles away from Sunland-Tujunga, where his *Mission Play* ran for 15 years. By 1927, the play had moved to a larger and more permanent home, now known as the San Gabriel Civic Auditorium.

McGroarty briefly summarizes key points:

> The historic mission play is a pageant drama presenting by means of both pageantry and stirring drama the sublime story of the founding of the white man's Christianity and civilization on the Western shores of America. Mr. R.D. MacLean, the eminent romantic actor, takes the part of Junipero Serra, assisted by over 100 players.

THE CHUPA ROSA RANCH. This name was chosen by John and Ida McGroarty for their home. The chupa rosa is an indigenous flower that attracts hummingbirds. The home later became the McGroarty Art Center.

JOHN AND IDA MCGROARTY. The couple is responsible for much of the social life and philanthropy of the town.

The first act depicts the heroic struggles and sacrifices of the Spanish pioneer to gain a foothold in California when they founded that mighty chain of Franciscan missions between San Diego and Sonoma. The second act depicts the missions in their glory when California was the happiest land in all the world . . . the third act tells the sad but exquisitely beautiful story of the missions in ruin.

On the advertising are these words: "How to get to Old San Gabriel—Take Pacific Electric Car leaving Sixth and Main streets, Los Angeles. Good automobile boulevard. Garage and automobile parking grounds adjoining the playhouse. Price of tickets, $1.00, $1.50, $2.00; box and loge, $3.00. All seats reserved."

Accolades on the bottom of the page: "I count the day I spent at the *Mission Play* as one of the happiest days of my life."—Thomas R. Marshall, Vice-President of the United States. And the words of Cyrus H.G. Curtis, publisher of *Ladies Home Journal* and *Saturday Evening Post*: "I lived in the joy and gladness of the golden age when I saw the *Mission Play*."

After touring California, Washington, and parts to the east, the show reached Chicago, where it folded. Plans had been for the group to go on to New York, the east coast, and to Europe, but McGroarty found that the farther the production got from California, the less interest the public showed. California's early history was not popular with easterners.

In its 23rd year, the play was closed after a 3-week run. Due to high production costs, with a cast of 75, two orchestras, props, and scenery, a 1950 attempt to revive the play following World War II was aborted. An era was ended, but the memory lingers on. It was McGroarty's charm and warmth as well as the work he accomplished that made him a beloved member of the Tujunga Valley Communities. He died in 1944 at the age of 82 years.

In the evening, it was good to dress up and have a "night on the town." In the Sunland-Tujunga valley in the summer of 1923, the Tujunga Valley Theater beckoned with adult admission at 30¢ and 15¢ for children. The theater was the "second building left of the old Tujunga Valley Bank building at Commerce and Tujunga Canyon Boulevard." The room could seat 360 persons. It closed during the Depression.

A printed theater program survives and tells us that one could see Norma Talmadge in *Smiling Through* or Helen Ferguson in *Hungry Hearts*. Later that summer, the features were *Mad Love* and *Back Home and Broke*, which included a Pathe Fables Cartoon. August 4 offered *Polly of the Follies*, which included follies, beauties, sweet patooties, vamps and villains, and homemade "fillums," all with Constance Talmadge and followed by an educational travelogue and a comedy, *Choose Your Weapons*.

The advertisers on the theater program were Tujunga Drug Company (everything at Los Angeles prices), Bloore's Dry Goods Store, Earl Brunner Jeweler (between the bank and the theater), and Darwin's Tujunga Sanatorium and Rest Home (electronic baths and violet rays).

According to the program advertisements, next door to the theater was The Sweet Shop. Johnson-Anawalt Tujunga Lumber Yard was just down the street. Leo L. Lang was selling real estate and insurance. Distillate and crude oil could be delivered at your door by Tujunga Oil Delivery. Milk and cream of quality were advertised by Hansen Heights Dairy, also to be delivered cold at your door.

The theater management promised satisfaction every day of the week with no disappointment: "Has Better Equipment for the Comfort and Protection of its Patrons than any other Theater in a Town of this Size," trumpeted one ad.

There were other theaters, live and film. In June 1931, The Tujunga Community Players Club presented *Its Great To Be Modern* at the Pine Street Auditorium. On June 9, 1933, the Tujunga Follies presented acts called *The Parade of the Animated Milk Bottles, Music of the Minuet, The Cake Walk, Bowery Waltzes,* and *The Two-Step*. There was a one-act comedy presented by the Tujunga School Teachers called *Twelve Good Men and True*.

On August 5, 1938, the new show house called the Tujunga Theater opened in the building at 6721 Foothill. Built by James Edwards Jr., it was the first of its kind in southern California. It held 850 people with an automobile parking lot adjacent.

Since that time, there have been many theater groups. Hundreds of films have been shown at the Tujunga Hilltop/Rainbow Theater. The John Steven McGroarty Auditorium at Verdugo Hills High School has been a popular location for shows. Unfortunately, the Rainbow Theater, as of late, is scheduled to be demolished. Also advertised on theater programs were the music and dances, such as a dance at Garden of the Moon to Jake Westner's famous jazz orchestra.

One would think, in those first years of the colony, that after a hard day's work, the Little Landers would consider going to a dance as just too much physical activity. During the day, there had been rocks to pile, fields to clear, animals to care for, and businesses to run. But the pioneers thought nothing of trudging up the hill from Sunland or down from the hills of Tujunga, carrying their lanterns to go to the dances held at Bolton Hall on a Saturday night.

When the Little Lands Colony was new, there were only about 200 people whose need for social companionship and entertainment was great. The small community developed musical groups. The 24-piece Monte Vista Band which, by 1915, played for many functions held in the San Fernando Valley, was considered a good advertisement for the community. A concert and box social given by the band in August of 1915 was considered a great success.

A private orchestra had played for the dances held on Thursday and Saturday nights at Bolton Hall. In addition, there were weekly parties for the Colonial Dancing and Social Club at which only colonial dancing was allowed. The membership of the club was 75 people. In those days, every man was considered

HILLTOP THEATER. An example of 1940s architecture, the Hilltop Theater was one of Tujunga's most modern. Built in 1938, it was severely damaged in the earthquakes. The front was demolished in April 2002.

MAYGROVE FAMILY BAND. The Maygrove family had a band which played at social functions in town. Gladys and Dorothy taught the men of the town to play instruments and read music.

a volunteer firefighter. Stories have been told about men in George Washington attire fighting a fire which had broken out during the dance.

Gladys Maygrove, a member of the Maygrove family band, wrote of her experiences as a young girl in town. One incident she relates, which happened at a dance at Bolton Hall, was the time when a fellow named Spence came to the dance, "and inside his shirt wrapped around his waist was a gopher snake. He frightened the girls out of their wits when he would let the snake stick its head through his buttoned shirt!" She added, "Another time at one of the dances during intermission we had an uninvited guest, a very large and hairy tarantula made his way slowly across the dance floor causing a commotion to say the least."

While the men were out taming the land, a young Gladys Maygrove was making a different contribution, that of providing music at Bolton Hall. She wrote the following in her memoirs:

> Tujunga in the early days was named Little Lands or Los Terrenitos with a small community of about two hundred people and we were much in need of a meeting place to hold our church services, our town meetings, also a recreation hall for school plays, dances, pot luck suppers, and our "box socials."
>
> Bolton Hall was the one and only place large enough to hold all activities in the valley. My mother, dad, eldest sister and I played for the Saturday night dances held in the hall. In those days the hardwood floors

Monte Vista Band. The band, pictured here in front of the fireplace at Bolton Hall, started small, but soon became one of the feature forms of entertainment.

> were smooth and shiny, the interior had no plaster on the walls, just the big boulders showing on the inside and the huge fireplace was a conversation piece itself.

The Maygrove family was a musical one. Walter, born in England in 1878, received his musical training from his father Joseph, beginning the piccolo at age 6, the violin at 9, and the piano at 12. When he was 10 years old, he was a bugler in the British army. After coming to the United States, he played at the old Pancakes Theater in Los Angeles.

After moving to Tujunga, Maygrove organized a band from "raw material," as he put it. The Monte Vista Valley Band was organized with men who knew little or nothing about music. Gladys remembers what it was like:

> On Monday nights we had band practice in the old Glorietta School House for anyone that was interested in joining. I remember my dad telling me to take any of the men aside that were interested in playing the trumpet . . . and I was to teach them the fingering on the instrument and also teach them the scale. My sister Dorothy would take another group of the men and do the same thing. I was only eleven years old at the time, but I had played in public many times, and had been playing the trumpet for seven years.

After many nights of practice, the band began to shape up so well that they were soon playing for affairs given in the Monte Vista Park in Sunland. That led to marching in parades. Gladys tells the following:

> One parade I remember so very well was the Prohibition Parade and the band marched the length of Broadway in Los Angeles, our "boys" managed well, due to the fact that they had already been put through the paces of marching around on the dirt roads near the school house. To play and to march at the same time is no easy thing to do.
>
> Each Saturday night a dance was held in Bolton Hall, with music provided by my family for dancing. Dorothy on piano, my dad on violin, mother on drums, and me on trumpet. Only square dances were held at that time and once in a while . . . the very new foxtrot would be thrown in. People came from all over the valley to attend those dances. They came in horse and buggies, or by Model T Fords, or they just walked the great distance.

The payment for the band for four hours of working and with a four-piece orchestra was $5.

One copy of a program tells about the entertainment enjoyed: Reading—Mrs. Leo Lang; Vocal solo—Miss Joe Akans; Cornet solo—Gladys Maygrove; Flute, piccolo, and ocarina novelty musical act—Dorothy Maygrove; Song—Dr. Buck; Baritone solo—Bing Maygrove; clarinet solo—R. Walter Maygrove; Monte Vista Junior Band (all under 13 years of age)—Star Spangled Banner.

Chan Livingston also remembered the dances. He said, "the high price in order to buy a box at the box social before the dance started at Bolton Hall was taking quite a bite out of our take-home pay."

As the years went by, new dances were choreographed and the music had a different sound. Maybe the on-lookers at the clubhouse watched the Charleston, heard the Big Band sound, and saw the Fox Trot and the Lindy. Dance pavilions were very popular at places like the Begue Ranch, the Garden of the Moon, and the lodges in the canyons.

One old-timer remembered an especially lovely time at the Saturday night socials in Bolton Hall when the lamps would be put out and the moonlight would come into the room brightly enough to illuminate the dancers in its soft light as the orchestra played "Good Night Sweetheart."

Early in the morning on April 1, 1923, the music of trumpets echoed from several points along the road that led to the newly finished Cross of San Ysidro, that same cross we now see above the McGroarty house in Tujunga. It was the first Easter Sunrise Service to be held atop Mount McGroarty. The trumpeters sounded their instruments at the first rays of the rising sun.

During one of the meetings of the Millionaires Club of Happiness and Contentment, the members got the idea that the community needed a landmark.

So, Marsh Hartranft donated an acre of land, dedicated to Mr. Pasco, an early minister of the Little Lands, and called it Pasco Park. The group made plans to erect a cross on that 2,000-foot-high piece of land. They dedicated the structure to John S. McGroarty.

One of the foremost citizens, artist George Harris, built the foundation. The cross itself is made of reinforced concrete poured in one continuous process. No wood was used.

The naming of the cross has great significance. It was named for San Ysidro, Patron Saint of Little Homes. The dedication service exhibited the attitude of the creators. Wallace Morgan of the *Record Ledger* wrote:

> The most significant evidence of the spirit of tolerance developed by the valley's pioneers was furnished by their first Sunrise Easter Service . . . By a special dispensation, Father Tonello, pastor of Our Lady of Lourdes Catholic Church of Tujunga, conducted the service of dedication. Members and clergymen from all Protestant denominations in the valley participated in the service.

The information about Ysidro came from McGroarty:

> The unusual feature of this religious cooperation was that San Ysidro, Patron Saint of Little Homes, in whose honor the cross was built and

THE CROSS OF SAN YSIDRO. Looking over the town from Mount McGroarty is this beautiful cross. The base was constructed by a local stonemason and the cross itself was dedicated by Father Tonello of Our Lady of Lourdes Catholic Church of Tujunga.

CROSS OF SAN YSIDRO.
Trumpeters were stationed along the
trail to the cross on the first Easter
Sunrise Service. San Ysidro is the
Patron Saint of Little Homes.

raised, was not a saint of the Catholic Church . . . nor, so far as known, was he affiliated with any Protestant denomination. He was a Spanish peasant, and his name . . . indicates he probably was a Jew.

San Ysidro's only claim to sainthood, it seems, was due to the love, gratitude, and reverence that he showed his neighbors and fellow peasants in the small Spanish community. He was given the title of Patron Saint of Little Homes by the common consent of his friends and neighbors.

McGroarty and the club members felt that the example of true kindness shown by Ysidro to his fellow man was the essence of the beliefs of the people living in the Tujunga Valley. Of the saint, McGroarty said, "We pray to God to let San Ysidro watch over our little homes and protect them and those who dwell in them."

Thus, the first Sunrise Easter Service in the Green Verdugo Hills was sponsored by an organization of laymen, held around a cross that was raised in

113

HILLS OF PEACE CEMETERY. *The bodies washed away in the flood of 1978 were reburied on firmer ground.*

honor of a "saint" who was probably Jewish, blessed by a Catholic priest during ceremonies involving all Protestant organizations in the valley.

From 1923, the cross has stood sentinel over the valley. In its first year, it was illuminated. The nightly lighting, costing $200 for the year, proved to be too expensive. After that, the lights were kept on for two weeks before Easter and Christmas. The Tujunga marker could then be seen from all of the Tujunga Valley and from most of the San Fernando Valley as well.

Beginning with the 1937 sunrise service, the Tujunga Kiwanis Club was involved in the sponsorship of the Easter services on the top of Mount McGroarty. At one time, during the 1950s, there were as many as 800 people at the services, watching the sun rise over the San Gabriels, listening to the music, and celebrating so many things. Some celebrants walk to the cross, starting out long before dawn, while others ride horseback. Most people take the shuttle provided by the Kiwanis Club beginning each Easter morning before daybreak from Hillhaven and Foothill, Tujunga.

The history of the pioneer cemetery Hills of Peace is bittersweet. The first group of settlers to be buried in that hallowed ground were the veterans of the Civil War and the local settlers. It is here that Old Pastor Wormon was buried, after asking Hartranft for the plot of land. During the 1930s, 1940s, and 1950s, the Tujunga Cemetery Association, with its custodian Mabel Hatch, operated and cared for the place. During the first 30 years, the people of the town volunteered work and expense. A Mr. Shersbey, who kept himself "in good physical trim," volunteered first. Hatch said that he put in three weeks of hard labor, bought his own arnica and liniment, and got an official vote of thanks.

It was in 1958 that the Hills of Peace Corporation took over the property and added the mausoleum. After only four years, the place was in a state of general neglect as vandals and weather had taken their toll. The graveyard had become a place for homeless people, robbers, and dogs, as well as a source of trouble for the police and an eyesore to the neighbors.

The ownership changed again in 1973 to the Institute for Christian Research, but by 1975, the plight of the graveyard was again grim. Its condition hardly matched the sign which read "Endowment Care, Sacred Grounds." There were still unsolved problems with graves, markers, and an odor from the mausoleum. By then, the cemetery had been used for the burial of indigents of Los Angeles County. In 1976, the remains of seven cremated bodies were found on top of a junk pile at the cemetery, left there by the vandals.

In 1977, there were accusations of dishonest dealings, false statements in contracts, misuse of endowment funds, and other charges filed against the owners, but the worst had not yet happened. It seems terrible, the desecration by vandals over the years. Time after time, graves were opened and bodies left exposed. The caretaker's house was looted and nearly destroyed. Piles of trash and the debris of vagabonds piled up. Weeds grew high over grave sites that had sunk into the earth. The mausoleum crypts were broken open. Bees drifted in and out of the vandalized crypts and marble covers were broken. A stolen Volkswagen and stolen car parts were found there. In 1993, two fires were set, burning 50 percent of the foliage on the grounds. In 1997, a discovery was made that teenagers had shattered eight crypts and opened several caskets. They left a woman's corpse propped up against the mausoleum with a cigarette sticking out of her mouth.

Even the vandalism was not the greatest threat. It was from the flood waters of 1978 that the greatest blow was delivered. January rains loosened the hillsides, so that February storms wrenched open graves and sent about 30 caskets slipping and sliding down into the yards of homes below or into the Parsons Trail roadway. One homeowner found as many as three bodies heaped up at the back door.

Skeletal remains trailed the hillside and as many as 55 bodies were eventually collected. After months of delay, the bodies were re-interred in a mass grave. In 1978, the cemetery was closed. From city funds, $200,000 were used to restore and shore up the hillsides and the cemetery.

It seems that the horrors of the underworld have not been the problem for the cemetery, but the threat of the upper world that is to be feared. Local citizens have been cleaning the place up and trying to find a way for it to be cared for. The group called "Friends of the Hills of Peace," with a board of trustees composed of four people, have taken temporary responsibility for the care of the 4,000 people now resting there.

It seems that the Hills of Peace have known anything but peace.

10. Recreation for the Naturalist

Work is usually relieved by recreation. Some of the settlers made their living by creating places for enjoyment. Often, if the land was not good for farming, it was used for another purpose.

There was a wonderful place to go in the 1920s on hot summer days when the work was done. In Monte Vista, a small lake had been dredged out on marshy ground that had been too wet for Edgar "Grandpa" Lancaster's cattle to pasture on. Lancaster, with a mule, a Fresno dredging device, and his own strength, created a shallow lake that became famous all over the Los Angeles area. Willow trees shaded a picnic area. As time went by, boats were provided.

Edgar F. and Margaret Lancaster had purchased 5 acres on that piece of low, marshy land next to Sunland (Monte Vista) Park in 1908. They first used the low, marshy land to make a reservoir and by 1925, the reservoir had been made into the small lake. Trout were stocked, about 500 in 1928. In 1931, a 1 1/2-pound catfish was pulled from the lake.

Lancaster Lake become the favorite spot for movie companies and recreational activities, attracting visitors from miles around. Lancaster would sometimes allow children to swim there. Girls could swim two days a week, boys the rest of the time. Family members were always on hand to insure the safety of the children.

It must have been a pleasant place. On a summer day, there would be a baseball game at Sunland park, a picnic under the oak grove, a concert, and a walk around the lake. Athletes from Sweden, visiting for the Olympics in 1932, saw their first baseball game at the park and enjoyed the lake.

In 1929, a motion picture was being shot there that featured a pet mud hen and six white swans. A year later, a "talkie" was filmed. They used the Tujunga Hotel to house the cast. Later, a movie starring Jackie Cooper was made, perhaps the infamous *Ben Hur*. Even before there was a lake on the property, a movie was made on nearby Lancaster pasture, using Lancaster's cow as a prop. It starred Mary Pickford and Charles Ray. In gratitude, Pickford donated a bell to be hung in the Baptist church in the Park which Lancaster had started. That bell is now in the First Baptist Church of Sunland.

The lake, fed by a spring, was surrounded by weeping willows. An arched bridge connected its two parts. The newspaper reported that over the Fourth of

July weekend in 1931, all the cabins were rented, indicating that people could stay there over night. A children's play area consisted of wooden "animals" fashioned from logs, including a horse, buffalo, pig, elephant, and camel.

One day a bobcat, rescued from a tree by Lancaster, was put on display at the lake house. A turtle named Isaac, who made his home on the shore in summertime, spent its winter months in a rawhide trunk in the "curiosity house." The lake animal collection could most likely be considered the first zoo in town. Outside, 51 species of birds could be seen at various seasons at the lake, according to the Audubon Society.

A merry-go-round made from cart wheels, swings, and other equipment made the lake an attractive place for children to play. Lancaster added some old coins to his museum. He displayed a 3¢ piece, a 1¢ coin dated 1853, and a 15¢ bill.

In 1949, Lancaster became ill and could not care for the property and, unfortunately, the water level gradually receded. The lake had been used for 25 years. After a flood control channel was built, a water pump on Sherman Grove supplied water to both the lake and Adams Olive Cannery on Wentworth. That pump could not supply enough water for both and by 1950, the lake was dry.

Recreation also consisted of walks and picnics along the river in the Big Tujunga Wash. People enjoyed the beauty of the yuccas, which are in full bloom in spring. These stately plants have been admired for decades, being called "The Lord's Candles" and "Candlesticks Of The Desert." The Yucca Whipplei in the

LANCASTER LAKE. Edgar Lancaster used his low marshy ground to make a reservoir, which he dredged out with a mule and a Fresno. It became a popular recreation spot for hundreds of picnics, boating, and sometimes for swimming.

Big Tujunga Wash is unique, being the tallest known, reaching reported heights of 20 feet. It is a thrill to stand beside one, look up, and realize its size.

There is a message in the story of the yucca, perhaps. The giant flower houses a small moth called the Prodnuba Moth, the only species to pollinate the flower. The female gathers pollen in a ball from one flower, visits another to deposit her eggs in its pistil, then rubs the pollen onto the stigma. This action insures that seeds will develop for the larvae to feed on and that the flower is pollinated. The moths have no other home. They cannot exist without each other.

Yucca's fibrous leaves have supplied man with material to make rope and baskets. The flowers and buds are edible and a drink is made from the fruit. This lovely, lily-like plant, which sends up an enormous spike of white bell-like flowers in early summer, dies after its great effort. Its roots send up new plants which themselves bloom after several years.

Besides the yucca, there are other living creatures unique to the 800-acre corridor that we know as "the Wash." The diversity of plant and animal life has made the area an outdoor laboratory with both mountain and Mojave Desert vegetation, plus the associated animals. Valuable scientific data is acquired by observing the adaptation of vegetation after the disturbance of frequent flooding. The ever-changing terrain and seasonal wetness, followed by rigorous hot and dry periods, have a unique effect on plant and animal life.

The plants have grown due to the extensive drainage area created as vegetation and animals move down from the mountains via Mill Creek and the Big Tujunga

THE YUCCA PLANT. Admired for decades, the tall cactus flowers have been called "The Lord's Candles" and "Candlesticks of the Desert."

BIG TUJUNGA WASH. For years, the Tujunga Wash was set aside as a nature reserve and priceless outdoor classroom. Everyone in town went to the canyon pools to cool off on those hot summer days.

River. In this small area, woodland plants exist with desert plants, next to alluvial scrub and chaparral. The endangered slender horned spine flower and Davidson's mallow, for example, are found only in isolated washes in southern California and grow abundantly in the Tujunga Wash. Manzanita and golden cup live oak can also be found.

A secluded other-worldly haven, the Tujunga Ponds, a small wetland area, is located within the Wash and is a designated wildlife sanctuary. The ponds provide a study area for school children, where one can see the egret and the great blue heron, quail, kingfishers, kestrels, and as many as 120 other bird species. In the Wash and the canyons, children of many generations have collected polliwogs, hunted for rocks, and splashed in the stream. To walk or ride horseback into the Wash is an experience common to the locals. From the road, the whole area appears to be a dry wasteland, but once on the sand and rocks, beneath the alders, among the willows and bushes, and beside the stream, there is peace and serenity.

Over the years, there has been much fighting over this Big Tujunga Wash. The land was set aside as a nature reserve and priceless outdoor classroom for over 40 years. It was hoped that the Wash would become a protected area under public ownership. In the years 1927, 1930, 1941, 1945, and 1954, citizen committees were formed to propose that the area should become a park. The Olmstead Report stated that it should be developed as a simple open landscape; the Haynes Foundation Report pleaded to keep open space in the midst of maturing urban growth; and The Rodney Report urged the use of the Big Tujunga Valley as a Regional Park.

In 1955, Sunland-Tujunga citizens organized opposition to additional gravel mining in the Wash. Again, a park was sought when in 1957 the Los Angeles City Recreation and Parks Committee asked that $250,000 of the Bond Funds go toward approximately 100 acres of the Wash. The question was raised once again the following year. Gravel mining, once an important local industry, flourished in the alluvial material of the Big Tujunga Wash, and it was the only commercial use of the flood plain. Sand, gravel, and rock were an important commodity in the rapidly developing southern California area.

From the time of the land boom in the 1880s, as the railroads expanded across the country, roadways were built and extended and great amounts of building materials were needed. The population increased. The Port of Los Angeles was built, flood control was provided, the California aqueduct was constructed, and airports and the freeway system were built. Building materials went from adobe, rock, and wood to concrete and asphalt.

For those living in the community for their health, the mining polluted the clean air of the people. A victory was celebrated when the Los Angeles city council voted to deny gravel zoning, a city action sustained by the United States Supreme Court. The Hjelte Report, in 1963, stated that "the public interest would be best served by leaving the wilderness area as it is." Due to the continuous efforts of citizens, in this great controversy, gravel mining is prohibited "forever" in the Wash. A golf course is now being considered for part of the level space.

There have been many requests to leave the Wash as it is. Of course, it will never again be in its "natural" state. And the river? It goes through its seasons of drought, flood, and an earthquake now and then, though it is neatly channeled along concrete embankments.

In addition to Sunland Park, Lancaster Lake, the Wash, and the Tujunga Canyon recreational area, there was another place close to the heart of every old timer and that was Pop's Willow Lake.

There were actually two Pop's Willow Lakes. Jack Wollard, who lived in Sunland in 1924, remembers the first "Pop's" very well. That first lake, which opened in 1931, was owned by "Pop" Gautier and was located in the Wash where there was an abandoned rock quarry about 30 feet deep in the middle. It filled with water from the natural stream to form the lake, always keeping fresh and clean-smelling because it was being constantly replenished by the flowing water. Because of that flow, there was no need for chlorine. Pop's was a wonderful place to go; there was a raft to swim to, picnic areas, an "Indian village" with tepees for the children, loud speakers, and music. There were trails to follow through the rushes and willows. People could take out fishing boats and canoes. Families spent happy hours joining with nature.

The flood in March of 1938 filled in the lake, practically wiped out the resort, and nearly closed it down, but, as the *Record Ledger* reports, "the owners went pluckily to work rebuilding it."

Several years later, the second Pop's Willow Lake was built on Orcas Avenue in Lake View Terrace, away from the flood plain. It had a shaped bottom of gunnite and was really a large swimming pool. The newspaper tells us that "Pop" Gautier, age 71 in 1951, celebrated the twentieth anniversary of San Fernando Valley's first fun resort by holding the annual bathing beauty contest, which handed out $100 in prizes. The beauty parade was judged by television and radio personalities and an actress.

Not many stories of the times at Pop's survive, but Jack Wollard remembers one. It seems that there were three life guards on duty all the time. Two of the men would occasionally jump into the pool to cool off and change sides. One fellow, though, never jumped in. It seems that he did not know how to swim. When asked what he used to do if someone was in trouble, he answered, "if they were drowning, I just threw them a life preserver." One fellow had a few beers and did a swan dive in 3 feet of water, a real catastrophe.

It is reported that in 1954, Los Angeles began accepting leasing applications for property adjacent to Hansen Dam, Pacoima, or Pop's Willow Lake, to use the Hansen Dam flood control basin for public recreation. That was the end of Pop's Willow Lake. The pool closed down partly because of too much "trouble" and too many drownings, as well as the pressure to yield the land to the city for a recreational area to be constructed at Hansen Dam. The first lake is more fondly remembered.

Filmmakers had been a part of the Sunland-Tujunga, Lake View Terrace, and Shadow Hills communities. Since the time of the silent films, locations in

POP'S WILLOW LAKE. The lake was a stream-filled rock quarry.

LANCASTER LAKE. In addition to being a popular recreation spot for locals and visitors, the lake was also the site of several films, including scenes from Tarzan.

Sunland Park, Lancaster Lake, and the Big Tujunga Canyon were popular sites. The Monte Vista Hotel served for housing. Verdugo Hills High School has nearly lost count of the filming at its location.

Some of the films, listed in a booklet written by Mary Lou Pozzo, are such notable titles as *In Old Louisiana, Our Gang Comedies, Coquette, It Happened One Night, Ben Hur, The Runaway Bus, Ernest Goes to Camp, River's Edge, Corvette, The Craft,* and *E.T.—The Extra-Terrestrial.* These films date from the years of the silent pictures of the 1920s, with stars like Billie Dove and Mary Pickford, to the modern blockbusters, starring Keanu Reeves and Dennis Hopper.

At Sunland Park, the 1941 Frank Capra classic *Meet John Doe* was filmed under the oaks. A set consisting of a small café was constructed in the area where the little rock monument still stands at the eastern end of the park near Sherman Grove. Gary Cooper talked to the young boys of the town at that spot.

A good part of the 1949 film *All The Kings Men* was made in Sunland Park, also. The pitcher's mound area of the eastern-most baseball diamond was converted into an old fashioned speakers platform, decorated with red, white, and blue bunting, from which Broderick Crawford made one of his famous speeches in his role as Huey Long. He earned the Oscar award for best actor for the part.

At Lancaster Lake, Ann Blythe was on location most likely for the 1945 film *Mildred Pierce.* In the late 1930s and early 1940s, many of the *Tarzan* series episodes were shot at Lancaster Lake with Johnny Weisemuller starring as Tarzan. One local resident remembers being very disappointed in Tarzan as he wrestled with a dead crocodile in the lake, the only motion of the dead croc being caused by

Tarzan as he flipped it back and forth. "He completely lost his hero status with me when he emerged from the water and a studio man rushed up and put a white robe over his shoulders."

The biggest production of them all was the fourth remake of *The Spoilers*, made in 1941 and 1942 in the Big Tujunga Wash. The filmmakers converted a huge area of the Wash at the bottom of Oro Vista into an Alaskan mining camp. Miners' tents were everywhere and a fake mine tunnel was dug back into the cliff at about the same location where the bridge over the creek to Riverwood Ranch now stands.

Several hundred yards of railroad track were laid and the climactic scene of the movie involved a real live train wreck. At one time or another, all of the stars were supposed to have been on the set, although I only remember seeing John Wayne. Also in the movie were Marlene Dietrich and Randolph Scott. Many kids cut school to see the train wreck scene.

Two of the last films made in Tujunga were *E.T.—the Extra Terrestrial*, filmed in the Seven Hills area, and *The Craft*, filmed in a Sunland home.

The list of films, commercials, made-for-TV movies, and television series filmed in Sunland-Tujunga are close to uncountable. Jaye P. Morgan should be on the list of famous people who lived in Sunland-Tujunga, as she was a student at Verdugo Hills High School. Other local celebrities in the entertainment industry who lived in town were the Smothers Brothers, "Nature Boy," "Big Chief White Horse Eagle," Ward Bond, Francis X. Bushman, Cecil B. DeMille, Leo Gordon, A. Martinez, Will Samson, and many others.

Down Commerce Avenue, at the highway, the Garden of the Moon flourished as one town party place. The Moon Festival comes to mind as the Tujunga merchants prepare for the new Commerce Street Fair, since this fair, held in October, takes place across the highway from the site where the Garden of the Moon once stood. Sadly, the Garden of the Moon was torn down in December of 1941.

It was in September 1921 that headlines in the *Los Angeles Evening Express* read: "Brilliant Tujunga Moon Fete . . . 15 Pretty Girls in Lively Contest to Be Queen for Festival," "Arrows Will Lead Motorists to Outdoor Carnival in Mountain Town," and "All roads Lead to Tujunga." The article describes what visitors could expect:

> There will be dancing in the spacious outdoor pavilion, an unique country store, a huge camp fire, community singing and a typical Indian dance has been arranged. There will be free parking tents for week-end visitors, full equipment and free water. Most important of all free admittance to the daily sessions of the Millionaires' Club of Happiness and Contentment, that group that is open to all neighbors of the sunny slopes, including the man who plays the flute, the man who reads the papers, the man who has the phonograph, and many others.

Special transportation facilities will be provided from Los Angeles, Pasadena, the Santa Monica Bay district, Glendale, Burbank, and other nearby cities. Preparations are being made for the accommodation of an unlimited number of camping parties, so that the ideal vacation trip up into the picturesque foothills of the Verdugo may be most delightfully combined with novel features which the moon festival will offer.

Later, a swimming pool was added and a dance floor with free picnic tables near it that was a quarter of an acre. "Free Quoit Grounds—Free Cooking Ovens" and "Bewitching Music—A Safe Family Resort With An Atmosphere Congenial to People of Culture" were also advertised.

One of the festivals must have been a big success, for the last entry in the news that September was, "Moon Festival of Tujunga Closes Amid Splendor." The last night featured a grand ball. Over 500 people signed the register of the Millionaires Club. Mary Begue was crowned queen. The conclusion of the report was, "The committee in charge backed up by every resident of the little metropolis has shown that 'it can be done.' "

At one time, there were also places in the canyons where people could go to have a good time. One of those establishments was the Pine Cliff Lodge in Big Tujunga Canyon, once located at the end of Stoneyville Road at Vogel Flats. The 160 acres of Pine Cliff Lodge was the largest privately owned land in Angeles National Forest.

GARDEN OF THE MOON. Built in 1921, the Garden of the Moon was a pleasant place under the oak trees and was popular all over the Los Angeles area. Every part of the garden was designed to be of comfort to the party crowd.

GARDEN OF THE MOON. *The garden was a centerpiece of the community and included a dance floor, swimming pool, and space for large events.*

Though the lodge, built in 1890, had survived many natural disasters—floods, earthquakes and forest fires—the famous historical building was destroyed not by a natural disaster, but by the blazing flames of a house fire in August 1975. It only took a few minutes on that Sunday afternoon for the fire to consume the wooden structure, leaving only the stone fireplace and chimney.

The *Record Ledger* published a lengthy report about the lodge on March 20, 1975, written by managing editor Tony Kiss, which gives us some information. He writes that the first construction on the property was a small shack on a homestead built in 1884 by the gold miner Silas Hoyt. Local citizens were trying to save the old ranch house. The forest rangers were trying to have the old structure burned down.

The owner, Walt Sanborn, and the United States government were at odds about the sale of the property. The rangers wanted the land to provide a park for campers. At that time, apparently, there were two opposing factions. There were those who were "the reckless destruction derby, played over and over again by modern day cultural barbarians" and those who wanted to preserve California cultural heritage.

According to Kiss, the ranch house, on approach, was simply overwhelming: "To the right of it was a small corral with a green, grassy meadow with trees in full bloom . . . there was a huge fallen oak tree etching a dark, skeletal silhouette against the blue sky. Old wagon wheels and small flower beds lent further, rustic atmosphere to this pleasant scene of tranquility around the old home."

Beneath the old oak tree was the very spot where great-grandpa Sanborn shot one of the last grizzlies at the turn of the century. The house, built in 1890, once served as a hunting lodge. In the 1920s, bands used to play at Pine Cliff and dances were held there. The chicken shed of 1975 was once used as a band shell and adjacent to it was the dance pavilion.

For a short while in the 1930s, the house was converted to "a house of ill repute." Scantily dressed girls could be seen playing cards with male customers or would be seen skinny-dipping in the nearby stream. "This enterprise was very short-lived though, it lasted only eight months and had succumbed to pressure from local Puritans," wrote *Record Ledger* columnist Tony Kiss.

About three miles above the ranch was a waterfall from which water was piped into the house. This is said to have been the very waterfall which earlier had provided an escape route for Tuburcio Vasquez, the area's best-known bandit, who was almost caught there by the posse.

At the time of the fire in 1975, the old building was in a state of neglect with broken shingles, sagging ceilings, and missing floorboards, but no damage that could not have been repaired. Opportunity for repair and revival did not come. Now all traces are gone.

PINE CLIFF LODGE. The lodge became one of the finest places to go in the 1920s. Located in the Big Tujunga Canyon, it withstood all the natural disasters that threatened.

11. Advancement for a New Age

The 1920s are well known as a time of revelry. The foothills were a good place to come for fun and liquor. The canyons were so far away from Los Angeles law enforcement that the sheriff was usually not close enough to notice what was going on. It was a good place to operate illegal stills as well.

Headlines in the *Record Ledger* from June 14, 1924 shouted, "Still Raided By Federal Agents," "Barrels of White Mule Are Poured Into Family Orchard," "More Story Is Coming," and "Constable McCarty Gets His First Close-up of Moonshine Still." The article reports the following:

> The peace, serenity and unblemished respectability of the neighborhood along Los Robles avenue, Tujunga, got a rude jolt last Monday afternoon when federal prohibition officers raided a still hidden in one of the Dr. Humphrey cottages at the foot of the hills, beat in the heads of an array of kegs and barrels and let an amazing quantity of "white mule" percolate into the thirsty sands.
>
> Three men, alleged to have been connected with the operation of the still for some two weeks past, were arrested, the supposed leader or chief owner in the illicit venture being carried away in irons.
>
> The raid followed a visit by Dr. Humphrey who came up from Los Angeles last Saturday to look at his property in response to a tip from neighbors that something queer was going on. For some days past the smell of the liquor had been standing out in more and more contrast to the odor of the roses and wild honeysuckle, and queer noises at night and queer visitors by day were attracting attention even of Los Robles avenue residents, who were noted for their strict and exclusive concentration on their own affairs.
>
> Meantime the liberated liquor flowed across the driveway into an adjoining orchard and irrigated a number of budding fruit trees, a thrifty young fig tree receiving an especially copious wetting.

One of the bootleggers was caught loading bulky packages and was quickly cuffed and shoved onto the backseat of a sedan. The officers filled a touring car

CHAPIN WAY HOME, 1929. This frame house is where the still was found. The smell of dumped liquor collided with the odor of roses and honeysuckle.

with evidence and left for Los Angeles. It is reported that about 2,000 gallons of mash and 20 gallons of whiskey were seized from that arrest.

In 1928, a larger still was found in a cave in the canyon. Deputies who had searched for it for months confiscated 200 gallons of liquor and 9,000 gallons of mash in 30 wooden vats. There was a concealed trap door and an electric signaling device to warn of the approach of officers.

There were other reports of illegal activity during the 1920s. For example, a home on Chapin Way housed a storage of illegal liquor. It was possible, however, to get the spirits you needed by legal means. Evelyn Burdge's father made his own quantities of beer for his wife, who needed the nourishment of the brew. He always had friends knocking at the door. He did make a bit for company, but, since he had a permit to provide only enough beer for home use, he never made an enterprise from it.

Lloyd Hitt, a pharmacist, told that in the days of prohibition, pharmacists were the only ones who could legitimately sell alcohol. The druggist's license, dated 1918-1919, authorized the holder "to use Spiritus and Intoxicating Liquors for compounding prescriptions upon the Prescription of any Practicing Physician."

In the 1920s, some worthless land was discovered by a developer in the desert-like area near the rock quarries north of San Fernando Road. The land was unsuitable for farming and was located in a remote area, overwrought with sagebrush and cactus.

One of the promoters who saw value in this land was "Pep" Rempp. He did not form a utopian colony as Hartranft and the Little Landers did. Instead, he established one of the first planned suburban tracts in the area.

In an article from November 26, 1981 by Jim Timmerman, columnist for the *Record Ledger*, we read that in the mid-1920s, some of the suburbanites looking for cheap land away from the city could find readily available building materials. Rempp and a number of Hollywood-based investors saw the opportunity in 1926 and, in about a month, the original 14 houses had been built in Stonehurst along Allegheny and Wealthea in what is now Sun Valley. Soon, the number grew to 50. Advertising claims stated, "City of Contentment" and "Stonehurst, where life is worthwhile."

One resident, Judy Camargo, who lived in Stonehurst for 56 years at the time the article was published, said that constructing Stonehurst was a fairly simple operation. A Native American man, Mr. Da Montelango, just picked up the rocks off the ground and piled them up. Those simple homes on cheap land gave many families the only way possible to own a home. The cost of a 2-bedroom house to the settler was about $3,200, complete with furnishings and a Model T Ford thrown in. Smaller homes went for $1,800.

Rempp envisioned a business district and a streetcar line coming to Stonehurst, but that never happened. The rock quarry owners would not allow the rail line across their right-of-way. Stonehurst was, and still is to some degree, an isolated neighborhood. It is unique, distinctive, and beautiful. But poor Mr. Rempp didn't do right by his creditors and landed in jail. Nothing is known about him from then on. A resident from 1935, Verle Iman, said that it took 10 years for titles to the houses to finally be cleared from the legal tangle caused by the developer's mismanagement.

Erma and Richard Rutan, in Jim Timmerman's 1981 article, described the community when they settled in 1947: "There was nothing between here and

STONEHURST. Simple houses on cheap land afforded many families their only chance to own a home. The cost was $3,200 with furnishings and a Model T thrown in.

Burbank but grape vineyards." They said that the stone walls at their house provided excellent natural insulation because of their thickness, about 36 inches thick at the bottom, tapering up to 12 inches at the top. Residents of the community added decorative walls, walkways, and additions to the homes with the abundant, large, and comely rocks on their land.

The story is much the same in all the communities started on once worthless land in isolated areas where poor folks could get a start. It bears mention that many of those old rock homes are still standing and in good condition after more than 70 years.

Dreams and big ideas got the men started. When the dreams died, the settlers kept on working and refining until the worthless land was worthless no more. The value in monetary terms has soared. The Stonehurst tract is loved and treasured still.

A fellow in Tujunga had built his stone home by himself. The builder Elmer Reavis was known as "The lone builder—The Bear With Big Boulders."

In the newspaper, it was written:

> that the Verdugo Hills still furnish both inspiration and opportunity for descendants of Robinson Crusoe who like to tackle the raw forces of nature single-handed is being demonstrated up on North San Ysidro street where E.S. Reavis is building a two story stone house with his own unaided hands.
>
> The kind of house Mr. Reavis is building is illustrated by the fact that the front of the fire place, including the mantle, is formed of only nine stones, the largest of which, the builder estimates, weighs about 1400 pounds and which completes the span above the fire place and reaches to the top of the mantel.
>
> Mr. Reavis rigged up a chain pulley and lifted this great stone in place unaided. Also, he hauls all the stone for the fire place and the walls from the upper end of his lot by hand. He rigged up a cross between a stone boat and a three-wheeled cart, the front wheel being a 10 inch wooden roller such as house movers use with an iron rod through it for an axle. The wagon looks as though it were meant for a giant, but Mr. Reavis is a man of less than average weight and height.
>
> The only time this single-handed builder has to call for help is when he sets the guide by which he keeps his walls perpendicular. He is so nearly blind that he cannot see the bulb in a spirit level.
>
> But his work is true, painstaking and even elaborate. A cement stairway to the second floor starts with a semi-circular sweep of stone wall, with one upright rock and a round cobble stone on top for a newel post. The soil pipes are recessed into the walls, and the fire place is fitted with a metal back with an air space behind it, fed with cold air from outside and discharging warm air through a register in the face of the chimney.

HOME OF BOB OLIVER. Oliver, one of the owners of the Record Ledger *newspaper, also owned this typical stone house.*

The walls of the first story are practically complete and Mr. Reavis is getting ready to start the fire place for the second floor. But he says he is going to limit the size of the rocks in the second story fire place to not more than a thousand pounds.

Today, many of the rock houses and cabins are scattered here and there among the newer, larger homes. There is great diversity in the community, as shown by the many styles and ages of houses and apartment houses.

The areas of Sunland, Tujunga, and towns close by are famous for the beautiful hand-crafted homes. The town is also noted for people who have always been considered "rugged individualists." These days, from any freeway, one can see houses from horizon to horizon. Most were built in tracts by professional builders. In the Tujunga Valley, the land of San Ysidro, Patron Saint of Little Homes, the houses show the history of those rugged individualists and creative dreamers.

The Phillips, for instance, built a stone castle with a battlement that stood 35 feet tall in the hills of Tujunga. They named it "Hy-Yan-Ka." Mr. and Mrs. Phillips once housed over a hundred turtles and provided a refuge for game and wild birds. From 1927 to 1947, they welcomed as many as 70,000 visitors to their home and had as many as 800 picnics there. The castle-like battlement was a local landmark.

Many residents built small woodframe cabins near the streams for a weekend getaway from the busy life of the city of Los Angeles. Small places were erected specifically for those people who settled on the slopes of Tujunga in hopes of the healing of lung and arthritic ailments. Other homes have been built that resemble the Moorish and Spanish styles, farm houses, even a Disney-like home. After World War II started, tracts of small, square homes were built to house the middle-class families who worked at Lockheed Aircraft Company.

From the beginning, homes have been wickiups and adobes, tent houses, castles and ships, stone homes and trailer homes, chalets and shacks. There were the two-story, frame farm houses, the weekend cabins, and the hide-aways. Today, the condos, apartment houses, and expensive modern developments with million-dollar views are on the hillsides.

Many homes built of stone can still be seen. Bolton Hall is a fine example of a sturdy, durable edifice built of stone with heavy lumber beams and doors. The home that the Rowleys built so long ago is still as marvelous as ever. A small home in Sunland was built of cobblestone and mortar and remains very lovely. The present owner has reported that with only the stones and no insulation, the house is extremely difficult to heat.

There was once a time when an ambitious man could build his own home without strict building codes, restrictive zoning rules, high interest on loans, insurance rules, or high property tax rates.

ONE BUILDING FOR MANY USES. *In a small town, one building could house many businesses. In this building is the library, the* Free Press *newspaper, and the photography studio.*

Every town that's worth its salt must have a library and both Sunland and Tujunga had one of their own. It was the year that dancers were dancing to "Swanee," "Avalon," and "Whispering" on Saturday night, going to church on Sunday, and reading the books they checked out during the week. The year was 1929.

The old grocery store building on El Centro Street just west of Sunset Boulevard (Commerce and Valmont) had been completely renovated and refinished like new. It was finally ready to become the Tujunga branch of the County Library, placed close to the community center of Tujunga.

The first library had been placed in a corner of Bolton Hall when the building was the Little Landers clubhouse. The books had stayed there because there was no better place for them. During those years, the facility was not used much due to lack of adequate shelving and because the use of the hall for other things made it necessary to crowd the library into a corner under the balcony.

For those in Tujunga, the Sunland Library was too far to go. Sunland Library had opened in 1913 and was a county facility. During the Depression, the library was threatened with closing. It was necessary to economize. Hattie McNabb came to the rescue and guaranteed payment of all bills. Her daughter Mary Louise Eberhardt agreed to serve as custodian without pay. Sunland merchants and citizens agreed to give monthly donations to pay rent and utility bills.

In 1937, a small salary was given to Eberhardt for her services and the city library resumed responsibility for the station. While Eberhardt was custodian, until 1951, the Sunland station was a busy one with an average circulation of 2,450 books and magazines per month. It was open just 15 hours a week.

When the community of Tujunga was annexed to the city of Los Angeles on July 1, 1932, the Los Angeles Public Library took over the County station. The Sunland-Tujunga Branch Library, a city-owned property, was built in July of 1952. From the day it opened, the branch served an estimated 20,000 people. The circulation reached 250,000 and there were 6,000 registered borrowers.

The first chamber of commerce, it has been said, was the volunteer group of men who once gathered around the Tujunga Post Office to wait for the mail. The good camaraderie of these men, "The Millionaire's Club of Happiness and Contentment," resulted in a forward-moving cohesiveness in the young Tujunga community as early as the early 1900s.

The Sunland Chamber spoke out in a news article by H.L. Morrill, the chairman. He pointed out that the Monte Vista Chamber, organized in 1916, was incorporated in 1926 with a charter. Morrill declared that it was difficult to picture the town's current accomplishments, but he still tried to make them known to the public:

> There are a few things that do stand out:
>
> Sunland Park is a monument. The defeat of the widening and paving of Foothill Boulevard through Sunland saved the property owners thousands of dollars, was later done by public funds through use of gasoline tax funds.

> Street lights were installed from Roscoe to the park without cost to property owners, the name of Wix Avenue was changed to that of Sunland Blvd.
>
> Sunland School was built, Hillrose and Oro Vista were paved using gasoline funds, the storm drain was built. The present Sunland sign was saved, which "represents an untold advertising value."

Chairman Morrill's proposed plans included a recreation area at Sunland Park, better transportation facilities, better streets and lighting, better fire protection, roadways, sewage disposal, and, with area-wide cooperation, general improvement of the community. The Tujunga chamber of commerce by-laws from July 1933 state simply that the chamber's "object is to advance the economic and social welfare of the community." Those early years showed that emphasis. Dues then were just $1 a year.

On December 11, 1920, the *Verdugo Foothills Record*, direct lineal ancestor of the *Record Ledger*, began. The "business office" was a desk in the open air beneath a live oak tree on Commerce Avenue and Greeley in Tujunga.

According to Carroll W. Parcher, who wrote a history of founders Wallace and Frances Morgan, the first office was just the beginning: "In that shady, sometimes chilly location, Frances M. Morgan, wife of the editor and publisher, accepted subscriptions and advertising while her husband Wallace alternately wrote editorials and news stories, and worked on the construction of the concrete building which was to become the paper's first permanent home."

The *Record Ledger* newspaper started printing in 1922. The *Record* was at first a 4-column, 6-page publication. However, as Parcher reported:

> It soon became the voice of the community and was eagerly awaited by its subscribers every Thursday morning at the general delivery windows of the Tujunga and Sunland post offices.
>
> In April, 1921, a semi-magazine form with 16 three-column pages was adopted and the name changed to *The Record of the Verdugo Hills*. In June, 1922, the publication was moved into the first unit of its new building. This was the first permanent business structure in the new community. It was built of thick concrete walls and heavy, hand made oak doors.
>
> Wallace Morgan's newspaper had the characteristics of strong editorial opinions on both community and national affairs and news columns devoted to the principal interests of the people in the town which was just emerging from its Little Landers era.
>
> The *Glendale News Press* and the *Crescenta Valley Ledger* in Montrose that covered the territory including Montrose, La Canada and La Crescenta was printed in the *Record*'s Tujunga plant. In the beginning, the editor of the paper did all the work of news writing, ad selling, subscription taking, type setting, page makeup, presswork and mailing.

The *Record Ledger* closed down in the 1980s.

Communication is vital to any community. The telephone was soon made available. At one time, before direct dialing, a phone call, particularly internationally, was a major event. The caller would say, "Long distance, please." The long distance operator would say, "Number, please." The caller would give the name of the person being called and so on. Here is an example:

"I'm calling Fred Dolphin, Meacham, Saskatchewan, Canada."

"Thank you. One moment while I connect you." (buzz) "Hello, Chicago, how is the weather today?"

"Oh, hello, California. The weather is lovely. And yours?"

"I'll connect you . . . "

Across the country, the operators would chat as they made connections. Then:

"Hello, Saskatoon. Yes, I'll connect you with Meacham," as Dorothy Moen stepped from her kitchen to the telephone company in her parlor.

"Hello, Meacham. How are you, Dorothy?"

"Oh just fine. California calling? Hello, California."

"Hello!" loudly—it's a long way to Meacham. "I'm calling for Uncle Fred to wish him a happy birthday."

THE RECORD LEDGER. *The newspaper served the local area for 60 years. It is because of the existing copies of this paper that the museum is able to find the history of Sunland-Tujunga.*

"Your Uncle Fred isn't home right now. He's at the curling rink. Would you like me to ring him there?"

"Yes, thank you."

It was not until 1918 that the Sunland Telephone Company was organized with 22 subscribers. The line was strung from Glendale with service limited to one and one-half hours morning and evening. The switchboard was in the home of whoever operated it.

By 1918, there was real improvement. The consolidation of two telephone companies made it possible to phone from Tujunga on either line without having to travel to La Crescenta to use the home phone lines. By 1922, the Sunland Telephone Company had a night operator on duty from 10:30 p.m. to 6:30 a.m. By 1939, growth of the town expanded to the installation of 1,060 phones in the 31 years of operation of the phone companies in the Tujunga Valley.

TELEPHONE COMPANY. At first, the telephone company went from living room to living room. Then, this beautiful telephone office was built.

12. Trouble in Deep Waters

On the upper slopes of the valley in Tujunga, there was a new neighbor moving in. Residents were not too surprised when, in the 1930s, they saw a harbor tugboat come to anchor in the middle of a lot on Samoa Street. They asked questions, of course, of the white haired captain of the craft, Charles Farr, but they readily accepted him as a member of the community. His stooped figure soon became a familiar one on the streets and on the deck of his ship.

The captain's story began as many others did. He had asthma. Captain Farr was an old man before he gave up the sea that he loved. He had been born close to the New York Harbor docks and the smell of the sea was strong in him; so, despite weak lungs and a tendency to asthma and against everyone's advice, he sailed for the seven seas.

Toward the end of his career at sea, Farr shipped aboard the *Warrior*, a seagoing tugboat built in San Francisco in 1884. In 1901 the *Warrior* was condemned as unseaworthy and was dismantled. The hull, pilot's lookout, cabin, and mast were given to Captain Farr, who had them hauled to Tujunga.

The asthma began to creep up on him, so he took the old *Warrior* on her last voyage and dropped anchor among the rocks and California poppies to "watch the sun go down."

As the years passed, the old boat became a sturdy and familiar landmark. The captain became more stooped and his steps less certain and then one night, the sun did go down.

The neighbors, it is reported, found the old man in his cabin, serene and untroubled, "as his ship sailed into its last port."

While it is true that citizens in Sunland-Tujunga never had to watch overhead lest ruined men be falling from skyscrapers, they were nevertheless greatly affected by the Great Depression of the 1930s. The people in the Tujunga Valley, a close community, gave much more than a dime.

An old and brittle copy of the *Record Ledger* from Thursday, July 21, 1932 holds a front page article: "Service Club Starts Fruit Canning Job . . . Tujunga Valley Service Club began canning fruit Tuesday for distribution next winter." The article described the situation:

> Donations of fruit which the club expected to get from growers in the San Fernando Valley have not materialized, but Frederick T. Stevenson, whose home is on Day Street, contributed a generous quantity of Satsuma plums, and a lot of apples were sent in by Phil Begue. Forty mason fruit jars have been donated to the club in response and the fruit received Tuesday was about sufficient to fill them.

The fruit canners pleaded for more jars and more fruit. Six women were ready to continue the work.

Scattered throughout pages of the *Record Ledger* newspapers are examples of groups, clubs, and churches dedicating themselves to helping the needy and improving the community. By 1928, 12 service clubs had been formed.

As early as 1920, the Council of Community Service of the State of California, which had purchased the old Monte Vista Lodge, had converted it to a home for undernourished children. McGroarty himself volunteered to pay $500 for necessary repair work. The Boy Scouts cleaned up and beautified the grounds.

At almost the same time, some Glendale Elks Lodge members built a cozy home for a Tujunga widow and her children, done in one day. All materials and labor were donated. The Tujunga Elks Lodge added the finishing touches the next day.

During those early years, a clinic for tubercular patients was established. A health school for children, funded by local service clubs, was started to build up children's resistance to the disease. The Tujunga Valley Service Club was organized with representatives from all the clubs of Sunland and Tujunga to provide relief for needy families who had been hit with a catastrophe. Baskets of food and toys were delivered for Christmas.

By 1932, there was a critical need for help for the needy, but welfare work was impeded by lack of funds when the Tujunga Valley Bank closed on January 15. Two of the largest depositors had withdrawn their funds. The Tujunga Valley Service Club responded by installing boxes and barrels in stores that would be handy for residents to use in depositing cans or packages of food. People donated generously.

Much of the 25 boxes of oranges, 2,000 boxes of peaches, and a good crop of vegetables were processed and donated. Hartranft offered the use of a large tract of land and paid the water bill himself for individual gardens for needy families.

Firemen repaired and repainted toys for children. The American Legion distributed dinners for Thanksgiving and Christmas. The Disabled Veterans ordered 400 Christmas trees to sell as a fundraiser. A baseball game at Sunland Park helped raise funds for Christmas baskets. The Kiwanis Club furnished a community Christmas tree.

Local anglers caught 900 pounds of fish, which was then donated to needy people. A 4-acre tract yielded 3,000 pounds of potatoes and 750 pounds of corn for the relief association. Ten tons of peaches were donated for canning. There were 436 families in Sunland and Tujunga who were receiving food and clothing.

AMERICAN LEGION FOOD DRIVE. Over the years there were many food drives like this one at Christmas.

The Los Angeles Land Chest, headed by Marshall Hartranft, requested army tents to house the homeless. It was proposed that land not under cultivation was assigned to destitute families.

A deer, run over by a motorist, was donated to a charitable organization. Deer were becoming scarce. Unemployed men were trimming trees, including the willows at Pop's Willow Lake, for firewood for those in need. The sewing room at Tujunga furnished work for those women who were heads of families. The average wage was $3.20 for an eight-hour day. Donations were made for repairable clothing and quilt fabrics.

The charitable outreach by service clubs, churches, and others has continued in Sunland-Tujunga and still, today, the hungry are being fed. Clothing, housing, and health care are available.

Ads such as this one, submitted by a concerned husband, E.P. Newton, for his wife, a social welfare worker in 1932, were common:

> . . . those who wish to call on the phone regarding welfare work to call . . . only between the hours of 9 and 12 in the morning, after 3:30 in the afternoon, and on Sunday and Tuesday not at all. The work that Mrs. Newton is doing for the less fortunate in Tujunga is very strenuous and a great strain on the nerves, and she requires a few hours a day to attend

BOULDER ON FOOTHILL BOULEVARD. *Torrential rains washed boulders down canyons. This particular bolder is from the famous flood of 1938.*

> to her family and more personal affairs . . . It is a matter of good public
> policy not to wear these willing workers out until the depression is over.

Life was difficult in the 1930s in more ways than a person wanted or needed. Nature itself turned against the community in the form of some of the greatest floods. Even though floods are a way of life in the foothills, and care is taken to avoid the deluge of water and flooding, great damage often occurs.

In Sarah Lombard's book *Rancho Tujunga*, there is a report of natural disasters. Lombard points out that before 1931, floods and fires were such common occurrences that little note was taken of them. Prior to the completion of the Big Tujunga Dam in 1931, a flood was recorded for almost all years with normal or slightly above normal rainfall.

The floods of 1884 and 1889 are always mentioned in the literature. The deluge of 1914 is classed as one of the worst in history. Because of the sparse population, little damage occurred; in fact, no mention is made of the Rancho Tujunga area. After the place was built upon, though, the times of torrential rains became more important.

There are several reports from people who experienced some of the big floods. One account comes from Marion Johnson, who lived in Big Tujunga Canyon during the 1938 winter rains:

> We had about a week of rain when there had been a cloudburst way back
> up in the canyon. We had another storm come right on top of that, so
> you had about 15 or 20 inches within a week or so. All the debris from

above the dam in the Big Tujunga came down to the dam. That raised the water level up so the water went over the dam.

You had a tremendous amount of water coming down. With rocks rolling, it makes an awful noise. You'd see trees that were at least 100 years old or more bob down in the water a couple of times and they weren't there anymore. It was just a big wall of water.

At least half a dozen people were killed. Because of the noise, the people at the CCC Camp got on higher ground, but the camp got washed out. The Wildwood Lodge and many houses were washed away.

The Johnsons had made small pools in the river and a picnic area close to the stream and those were washed out.

Airplanes were used to supply food to the people stranded. Some people came out of the canyon on horseback or walked out, but people whose homes were intact stayed to take care of animals. Food was dropped for them.

Johnson continues, "About two weeks after the flood, they took one of the biggest bulldozers that you could get, put a flatbed thing on it and went up the canyon to get people out. The bulldozer went in to level the ground to make a road. Everybody's car or truck was behind this bulldozer which pulled us across where the streams were." There were about 20 places to cross the stream.

The rescue operation, however, displayed real community and cooperation. The news report states, "Due to the raging torrents and washout of roads and trails, many of those who were in the mountains when the storm struck were unable to escape for several days, and in the meantime were in dire need."

Hungry men were marooned in Big Tujunga Canyon, holed up in two sheriff's boy's club camps. Twenty-four men and women were at the Wildwood Lodge and

FLOOD DAMAGE. Homes and businesses were washed away or covered with mud.

32 were at the ranch of Deputy Sheriff Harry Pulfer in Trail Canyon. Twenty homes at La Paloma and Vogel Flats were destroyed, as well as 67 of the Department of Water and Power spreading basins. Nineteen men were marooned in a barn. Thirty others were known to be isolated in the canyon with limited food supplies. At the south end of the canyon, at one camp, 200 men working on a state relief project were cut off and their lodging washed away.

A plan was set in motion. The newspaper tells of the private planes manned by volunteer aviators:

> with no thought of reward, carrying a pilot and an observer, set out to survey the canyons and mountains. Flying about 2,000 feet above the ground they attracted the attention of the people stranded below. They then dropped messages fixed to a weight with a piece of red cloth attached.
>
> The message was that the aviators, from the sheriff's aero squadron, could drop a limited supply of blankets, food, clothing, medical supplies, matches and candles. They promised to return an hour later. The procedure, spelled out to those marooned below, was this: "Use strips of white cloth about a foot wide and ten feet long, placed on the ground in the open to form letters of the following code;
>
> 'A' means no help required today, return tomorrow. 'E' food needed at once for ten persons; 'H' food for twenty; 'K' food for thirty; 'L' food for forty; "T" food for fifty; 'V' first aid kit urgently needed; 'X' medical aid urgently needed; 'O' no casualties in our camp; 'Y' followed by a number indicated number of casualties in camp.
>
> If cloth permits, place all letters at once. Otherwise change as soon as definitely seen by pilot.

FLOOD DAMAGE. *Of the natural disasters, floods have caused the most damage.*

The plane would circle as needed. Packages were dropped in all the local canyons and mountain districts that could not be otherwise reached. All bridges in Big Tujunga Canyon were torn down and "a six foot head of water is running down the canyon."

The rescue operation was done under the direction of Sheriff E.W. Biscailuz with the assistance of the United States Navy. The supplies themselves were furnished by various relief organizations.

By 1941, the canyon had hardly built back up. The 1941 flood washed everything out again.

Hansen's Lodge was so heavily damaged that it was never repaired. Many cabins were washed away or covered with landslides. There were six known dead among the residents of the canyon. All local schools were closed for a time. There have been great rains and washouts since then, but with the precautions of the dams, debris basins, levees, and storm drains, the city has made a valiant effort to protect itself.

Over the years, Sunland and Tujunga residents have had to work together in many ways to overcome adversity. Neighbors in small communities mean a great deal to each other as they get through the difficulties of life. We can see the example of that in the residents of Trail Canyon.

It is said that the canyon was named Trail Canyon not because it was some footpath, but because there was a trail of gold dust in the gravel of the canyon's creek bed. (That trail was worked in the early 1900s, but played out quickly.)

It was a beautiful place, they say, with steep canyon walls, a creek, and a waterfall. In dry years, it was quiet, but during storms could be a raging watercourse. Fires have smudged it black. Mud filled its homes in 1938 and again in 1978 and 1979.

Irma Ward's stories tell of a childhood in the Big Tujunga Canyon area, Trail Canyon, and Mesa. There was the problem of transportation. The community was separated from the town by a 7-mile unpaved road. The "clay hill" (part of the road where Seven Hills Ranch is now), a dirt road that was very slippery in wet weather, is a memorable feature. Sometimes, their car would slip and slide to a drop over the side. The parents drove the road four times a day. When the car got flooded, one of the men would piggy-back the children to dry land. The children had permission to be excused from school instantly on rainy days when their parents arrived at the school.

There was terrible wear and tear on the car from the rough roads, so Mr. Pulfer, a good auto mechanic, kept many cars in running order. If one car did not start, all the children would pile into another one and go off to Sunland School or Verdugo High. On the way home, if the car could get across the first crossing, they could hike the rest of the way home.

Isolation was not troublesome for the children. A playhouse was built. There were table games, musical concerts, and a horseshoe pit. Some of the children wrote and circulated a newspaper. Articles were typed up about the weather. There was a report of a new radio in the neighborhood and a plan for a hiking party. Also, "Uncle Jack made a new ditch so the water wont warsh the road out . . . Mrs. Pulfer had a birthday . . . Lady Mac Phie has learned to sit up for her breakfast . . . Waters fox has gone to fox heaven." Then later, the sad report: "Lady Mac Phie fell over the bridge." The first edition of the *Tiddly Wink News* was released December 3, 1933.

The innovations used by the people were intriguing. One house had a solar hot water heater (an old water tank painted black) on the roof, which provided hot water in the afternoons and evenings on sunny days.

Because of the need for school transportation, it was possible to get an increased amount of gasoline during the war over the 4-gallon-per-week allotment. For fear of being stranded in Trail Canyon, one man buried a 50-gallon drum full of gas behind his cabin. He never had to use the supply. When they dug up the drum after the war, they found it to be bone-dry. There had been a microscopic leak in it and all the "reserve supply" had leaked out over the years.

The Trail Canyon Mutual Water Company distributed water from the stream to "Mr. Lowe's cabin on lot 31 and to all lots downstream from Mr. Lowe's place." Water was collected in a subterranean dam in the stream bed between lots 32 and 33. After going through a sand filter, it was piped to cabins downstream. Pipeline leaks were common, so pipeline repair work parties would mend pipes regularly and clean out the dam.

After a long, thrilling drive up the rugged Big Tujunga Canyon Road from Sunland, a surprise turn-out emerges on the left side of the road. One can view the Big Tujunga Dam from an overlook and there is an information board placed there by the rangers.

That dam has been holding back flood waters for over 70 years, a silent guard against the flooding that once destroyed people and property, spoken of as the "recurrent torrents of destruction."

The Big Tujunga Dam drains 82.3 square miles of mountain watershed (figures vary from source to source). There is a huge semi-circle of high country from the slopes of Mount Gleason, past Mt. Pacifico, and the table lands of Horse, Charleston, and Barley Flats, which provide the first water, allowing it to drain through narrows into the dam.

The first dirt moved from Big Tujunga Dam was on February 25, 1930. Los Angeles County Supervisor Henry Wright and Angeles National Forest Supervisor William Mendenhall were two of the men who hoisted the first shovelful of soil. E.C. Eton was the chief engineer of the project and L.E. Dixon Company was the contractor. Big Tujunga Dam, 13th in the district, was built with 1924 flood-control bond issue dollars. The cost of this structure when completed came to 80 percent of that estimated, quantities and cost, in the amount of $1 million including fittings (*Western Construction News*, May 1931). The structure was completed in 1931. The dedication luncheon, attended by over 200 guests, was held in May of that year. A ceremony included the christening of the dam with a bottle of lemonade.

FLOOD RESCUE. Rescues on foot were a difficult, lengthy process. Men from the camp for indigents in Big Tujunga Canyon were rescued during the flood of 1838.

It was thought that such a massive undertaking would lead to the elimination of a flood threat, but in 1938, even the concrete mass failed to control the fury of nature. After a night of drenching rain, the flood boiled over the spillway and a wall of water 15 feet high poured over and through the canyon. The flood destroyed or damaged everything in its way, including 447 cabins. Since then, the dam has contained the worst of the flood waters.

Figures are different in the various reports. The following information is quoted from the sign at the overlook provided by the Forest Service:

> The floods of 1938, 1969 and the earthquake of 1971 failed to register significant effect on the structure. During peak flows in 1969, an estimated 7,720,000 gallons of water per minute swept over the dam's 122 foot wide spillway. That year raging storm waters also carried with them 4,430,00 cubic yards of debris which accumulated behind the dam.
>
> The dam is a variable arch dam and contains 79,293 cubic yards of concrete. At its crest it is at an elevation of 2,304 feet above sea level, 200 feet above the original stream bed and 505 feet in length. Big Tujunga Dam has a maximum reservoir capacity of 6,240 acre feet.

And, according to the information in *Rancho Tujunga*, the book by Sarah Lombard, the structure is 75 feet thick at the base and 15 feet at the top. It rests in bedrock some 50 feet below the floor of the canyon.

A 1992 report states that during the rains of that year, the water came within 5 feet of spilling over the dam's rim. During torrents of rain, the reservoir has a capacity of 2.4 billion gallons. During drought, the water levels have dropped until there was more mud than water.

In 1968, there was little water. The reservoir was filled with an accumulation of silt and debris built up over 37 years to an estimated 50 feet. At an estimated cost of $3.7 million, close to 5 million cubic yards of deposits were moved out. Robert Blechl, reporter for the *Foothill Leader*, wrote that there must be a minimum amount of water to protect the valves of the dam and that a minimum of 1,484-acre-feet of water must remain.

The discharged water is distributed in various spreading grounds downstream. The value given to the conserved water was stated to be $3,250,000 annually.

In October 1998, the Big Tujunga Dam was brought up to state seismic safety standards with an $11.9-million grant from the Federal Emergency Management Agency (FEMA), that amount to be shared with four other dams.

Big Tujunga Dam. The dam was completed in 1931 and successfully held back flood waters.

13. In Recent Years

In the edition of the *Record Ledger* from December 18, 1941, a headline reads: "Plan to Intern 250 Japanese Aliens In Tuna Canyon CCC Camp—Bunk Houses Are Enclosed With High Fence." The location was approximately where Sister Elsie's goats once were and where the Verdugo Hills Golf Course is now. During the week preceding that date, workmen had prepared the CCC camp to serve as a camp for "alien enemies" taken into custody by the FBI. Men from the Department of Immigration and Naturalization were hurriedly completing the organization of guards.

The buildings at Tuna Canyon camp included four large dormitories or bunk houses, a mess hall, a library, a recreation room, a work shop, a barber shop, a tool house, two shops for repairing cars and trucks, a blacksmith shop, a shower room, and two large garages for the storage of cars. All were enclosed by a 12-foot, heavy woven wire fence with strands of barbed wire on top and electric lights placed at intervals to aid armed guards in frustrating any attempt at escape. Bolton Hall Docent Evelyn Burdge remembers that the camp was built around 1935 for the Works Project Administration (WPA) project. The relocation assignment was begun around 1942 and continued for the duration of World War II.

The *Record Ledger*, in April of 1942, reported, "Among the thousands of Japanese who, because of the war were required to leave their homes and occupations . . . [many] will be remembered by their neighbors and associates with the kindliest feelings and full confidence in their loyalty to the land in which they were born."

One Japanese family who lived in town was the family of Mabel Tsumori Abe. Abe remembers those war days well. She was about to graduate from Verdugo Hills High School that year and had been an honor student. She had earned a scholarship to the University of Southern California. She was active in school in "everything," she says: Explorers, Safety Committee, Poetry Club, Art Club, and the Girls Athletic Association (GAA).

Abe's father George owned and operated three produce stands, including one in the Foothill area. In addition to his regular work, he helped the FBI as an interpreter and was expected to be available at any hour. Mabel's brother Paul was a highly respected young man. At 12 years of age, he had become one of the most faithful and dependable of the boys in the Boy Scout Troop of Sunland and had

1940S INTERNMENT CAMP. Once a Civilian Conservation Corps (CCC) camp, this facility became an internment camp in 1941.

acted as color guard. Paul had been one of the Boy Scouts who stood watch daily at the air-raid observation post, "helping the devoted band of unpaid volunteers who had performed that vital service since Pearl Harbor."

The Abe family did not stay at the La Tuna Canyon camp. They were sent first to Merced, then to Colorado.

The night the Abes left town, scoutmaster Jens Knudsen went to say goodbye to the family just before they were evacuated. Quoted from the newspaper: "As he was leaving Paul's mother slipped a sealed envelope into the scoutmaster's hand, saying, here is something to help with the Red Cross trailer the Scouts are building. The envelope carried a $10 bill, the first cash contribution the Scouts have received for their project."

In the *Record Ledger* from March 26, 1942 is an advertisement:

> Thank you. During the past five years I have been honored to have had the privilege of serving you. I am now leaving for the duration of the war, and wish to assure all of the willingness of myself, family and clerks, to do our part to aid the United States in this conflict. It is my desire to return to Tujunga and serve you again. I thank all of you for the business you have given and the kindness and consideration you have shown me. S. Tsumori

Mabel Tsumori Abe's first graduation was in a camp. The family returned to Tujunga three years later where Mabel found clerical work, later married, and raised three sons. One of them is now a major in the Marine Corps. Her dream of graduating in formal ceremonies did come true, though, 56 years later. It was

June 18, 1998 that she marched to "Pomp and Circumstance" onto the football field at Verdugo Hills High School.

It must be said that the land on which Sunland-Tujunga is situated is overly abundant in natural disasters. Floods are common. Winds blow down trees and rooftops. Fires have been known to rage for days and months. Earthquakes have ripped roadways and tumbled buildings. Fire is one disaster that every citizen is familiar with.

It was August 1947 when smoke billowed yet again over the mountains. A 15-year-old boy watched the fire from his backyard on Oro Vista in Sunland. Tom Gilfoy told me his version of the story in October 1999:

> I watched the fire burn . . . as long as I could stand it before I decided to go see if the Forest Service would accept me as a volunteer firefighter. In those days they used to make appeals over the radio for volunteers and I had heard such a broadcast . . . I wasn't at all sure if they'd believe me about my age and told them I was the minimum required age of 18.
>
> We had a small farm and I had been left in charge for a few days when my parents left on a short vacation . . .
>
> Finally, after talking a neighbor into coming over to milk the goats, feed the rabbits and chickens . . . I hitched a ride up the canyon to Vogel Flat where the USFS [United States Forest Service] had established the fire camp. I remember what a terrific beehive of activity it was with fire trucks and firefighters whirling around everywhere. I was able to convince them about my age . . . the first thing they did was to issue me a blanket and tell me to go lay down under a tree and try to catch some sleep.
>
> Early the next morning while it was still dark they woke me and a whole bunch of other volunteers and loaded us into three stakeside trucks and away we went back down the canyon. In those days the road in the bottom of the canyon ended somewhere near Vogel Flat, so the only way we could get out front of the fire was to go round the other way.
>
> This meant going down to Foothill Blvd to Little Tujunga and from there to the old truck road to Pacoima Canyon which eventually ends at Mt. Gleason. It was while coming around a bend on Iron Mountain that a tragedy happened.
>
> I was in the second of three trucks and we had been eating the dust of the first truck the whole way. As we came around a corner I caught a glimpse of the first truck as it left the road and plunged over the side into the deep ravine below, throwing bodies out of the back as it tumbled its way down.
>
> There were several firefighters who had jumped or had been thrown onto the roadbed who didn't appear to have been hurt at all. But the rest, as many as 20, were either killed or were pretty well banged up. There were moans and screams of pain coming from all over the hillside.

149

Then, just to make things a little worse, the guy next to me in our truck started to have an epileptic [seizure]. I sure as hell didn't know what to do as he fell down on the truckbed and started shaking all over . . . a couple of us grabbed him and held him still while someone else forced a stick between his teeth.

This all happened in an instant and before long we were all out of the truck and helping bring the dead or injured back up to the road for evacuation. It's funny but I don't specifically recall helping with any dead bodies.

Gilfoy researched the fire and was able to find, in the August 8, 1947 issue of the *Los Angeles Times,* a reference to the truck accident he witnessed. It says in the article that there were 26 occupants in the truck when it went over the edge, but that they narrowly escaped death when the vehicle went off the road and landed wheels-up in thick brush. Thirteen men were injured, four seriously, while others suffered brush burns and other minor injuries.

The fire eventually burned off most of Mount Lukens, then jumped the canyon and burned its way out of control up Trail Canyon on its way to Mount Gleason. Because of the incident, the volunteers turned around and went back to the fire camp and were released to go back home without ever lifting a finger to fight the fire. Gilfoy says, "One thing I remember for sure is that we got paid from the time we signed in the night before until we signed out."

From the time of one great destruction in 1919, each report of a brush fire shows fewer and fewer numbers of acres burned. In one case, firefighters outside their station many miles away on a break saw the smoke, called in the alarm, and vehicles were dispatched within seconds.

In contrast, a 1925 report was made about a war on flames: "The orchestra was playing 'Red Hot Mama.' " The men were "blithely swinging their partners around the dance floor at the Garden of the Moon, Tujunga. Everyone was joyous. The musicians were at their best and the floor had never been smoother." Three deputy fire wardens made themselves known. The harmony died away in a last, long screech of the saxophone. A bundle of dusty shovels was thrown with a clang to the floor. Nearly 30 dancers were drafted to aid in the brush fire then raging in Big Tujunga Canyon, along with "two-score other men from the La Crescenta and Tujunga districts," who were taken by truck to the blaze.

Incidentally, prior to 1950, water supply was a problem. Old timers can remember when they had to bring water from other parts of town in buckets, the faucets being dry. The fire alarms are, for Tujunga, pretty sophisticated. In the early days, the job got done with a little more effort, but still effectively. A *Record Ledger* article tells of one instance:

On July 26, 1923, a Tujunga restaurant burned. At 1:15 a.m., Dr. Stella Conner, who was asleep in her home 75 feet away was awakened by crackling of fire.

Looking through an open window by her bed, she saw the flames and immediately began yelling "fire," first from a window on the east and then from a door on the west. A neighbor heard her call and fired three shots from a revolver in the air, and Orler Segner, next door, spread the signal for help with a few blasts on his bugle.

The Glendale Fire Department responded and made a fast run from Glendale in less than 20 minutes.

During the 1940s, citizens of the joined towns of Sunland-Tujunga enjoyed prosperity, jobs at Lockheed Aircraft Industry in Burbank, and a housing boom for those workers moving in. Vineyards in Sunland were converted to tracts of houses. The new group was filling the schools and churches, helping with the war effort, burgeoning the ranks of service clubs, and creating a need for small businesses to emerge.

The war years created a different atmosphere. The internment camp for Japanese, Italian, and Polish aliens was converted from the old CCC Camp on Tujunga Canyon Boulevard in the Begue and Fehlhaber neighborhood. The California State Mounted Militia, a civilian unit, was formed to patrol the area and ease any panic caused by enemy attack. The militia used the Big Tujunga Wash as a practice ground. Air raid wardens patrolled at night. Lockheed was covered with camouflage with assistance from the film studios. Water tanks were also

FIRE STATION, 1927. *Chief Harry Rice stands beside the new fire engine. The fire department was instrumental in helping keep the town together during the Depression and the numerous fires that threatened. The fire station shown here was built just behind Bolton Hall.*

camouflaged. Rationing was in full force and the men were away in the war. The women went to work at Lockheed and the world was changed. Keeping in mind that the Pacific coastal areas were most vulnerable to attack, the war at home was visible in California.

The 1950s were the boom years for business. Women were at home again to do the shopping locally. Churches were full to overflowing and large sanctuaries were built. At least 20 churches of all faiths met the religious needs of the people. There were 120 service and social organizations. Social life was rich with the school and church as the social center. Recreational activities were available for "good clean fun." The land had changed from an agricultural paradise to a bustling subdivision of Los Angeles, that once-sleepy pueblo.

As boundaries disappeared, everything from the mountains to the sea became homes and businesses on every parcel of land. Even so, there has been and still is an isolation that buffers both the big city life and deprives the area of adequate representation. Some say that Sunland-Tujunga is a forgotten part of the city. The land which was a part of the old rancho is still known as one of the few places in the city of Los Angeles specifically designed as an area for keeping horses and with maintained bridle trails.

Then, as always, the foothills were home to artists, writers, composers, musicians, actors, all people involved in the arts. The beauty of the mountains, the air, the seclusion, and the proximity to studios have always been factors for those

HOBER'S SUNLAND PHARMACY. *Opened in 1939, the store was the first drug store in Sunland. Besides the pharmacy, there was a soda fountain and all sorts of items for sale. It was moved and renamed Hober's Pharmacy and remained in business until 1995.*

MAIN BUSINESS DISTRICT. *This photograph shows Sunland's main business district until 1953.*

working in the entertainment industry. McGroarty's home is now McGroarty Art Center and is the place where children and adults learn painting, pottery, music, and other arts.

During the 1940s and 1950s, the sanatoriums were still in operation, one of which was the Sunair Home for Asthmatic Children, which was still quite famous. The first effects of smog were felt in the 1950s and many of the sanatoriums were gradually closed. Sunair lasted into the 1970s. Smog caused many changes, in fact. Before that time, there had been several fire lookout towers in the hills and mountains. They were closed for no other reason than smoke from a brush fire could not be seen through the brown haze. For a community once known for its "healing ability," the change was most unfortunate.

Recreational areas, such as the lakes and the carnival in Sunland Park, became rest homes, apartments, trailer parks, and commercial buildings. Even now, in the trailer park that was once Lancaster Lake, a small year-round spring flows. The olive industry closed down and moved north. Large land holdings shrunk to homes on small plots of ground. Thankfully, in the 1950s, the crime rate was still very low.

In April 1965, the Los Angeles City Planning Department issued the "Completed Plan for Sunland-Tujunga." In the introduction to this report, the concept presented was a word-picture stating the nature, function, and form of tomorrow's Sunland-Tujunga-Shadow Hills plan. It would clarify policies and long-range objectives.

See's Barber Shop. The shop was to move to another place. The men of the town put signs in the window and staged this picture.

The synopsis stated in part that "with its wide range of housing facilities, attractive light industrial plants, and beautiful Tujunga Basin, now reclaimed and channelized, it is considered a wonderful place to live." By then, the new freeway system was inching closer and had reduced isolation and accelerated economic growth. They noted that nowhere does a tall building obstruct the panoramic view. Of great importance to the future was this statement by a community activist: "Let's eliminate the traditional image of low income, haphazard development, etc. . . . this community has developed in a hodge-podge fashion. Let's eliminate the mess." Another voice cried, "The Sunland-Tujunga area should be renamed Verdugo Hills . . . Tujunga is difficult to spell and pronounce." The citizens wanted to continue to be a low-density dormitory suburb of Los Angeles.

The 1960s saw the beginning of a minority presence as school busing began and young people of all ages and races populated the schools. The move to home ownership by "minorities" began in the place that was touted 30 years before to be a "white only" community. Drug labs made their appearance in the hills and on wheels. Bikers and hippies moved into the hills.

Because of continued effort, the community at the west end of the rancho is still an equestrian community. In 1967, there were 120 service and social clubs still operating, as well as 900 businesses.

154

With the opening of the Foothill Freeway, the 210, in July 1972, a major change began immediately: people discovered that Sunland-Tujunga existed. With easy access and departure by way of the freeway, crime increased dramatically. One drug store, Hober's Pharmacy, which had no armed robberies since 1939, experienced nine armed robberies from 1980 to its closing in 1995. The sentimentality, romance, and camaraderie of the village and the colony began to disappear. Gangs vandalized and defaced property with grafitti.

During the decade of the 1960s until the present, the changes have occurred in two ways. The original small businesses have closed, leaving buildings empty. New immigrant groups have taken over the small business trade, pumping life back into the community. Because of a newer population, the sense of close community has changed. Single-family dwellings have become apartment houses and the people come and go, not becoming a part of the whole. There is a strange mixture of poorer people and those who have purchased homes for $500,000 or more for newly-constructed hillside properties.

Today, the Tujunga Valley blends into parts of the San Fernando Valley, Glendale, and Los Angeles. Over the hills to the south are Burbank, North Hollywood, and Van Nuys; to the west are Sylmar, Pacoima, and San Fernando; to the east are La Crescenta, La Canada-Flintridge, Pasadena; and to the south is the Los Angeles Civic Center—14 miles away.

Disasters have been prominent as a part of the growth of the towns. It is the moments of vulnerability that are remembered and that bring people together. In southern California, the stories about fire and earthquake are numberless. In the present, not much is said about the scorpions, rattle snakes, mountain lions, bears, stony soil, or dried-up water holes.

Growth and change are a natural part of life. This village that once was Monte Vista and Glorietta Heights, the Little Landers colony, Tujunga Terrace, and Hanson Heights have all become an open part of greater Los Angeles. The land grant once called Rancho Tujunga is huddled along the base of the San Gabriel mountain range on the edge of rugged wilderness, leading over the roads which follow the earthquake fault lines into the Mojave desert.

The area is also known as the gateway to the Angeles National Forest, a vast recreational area. In 1971, and at other times as well, the hope was to seek a recreational identity. So, citizens began a plan to develop the Big Tujunga Canyon, the Verdugo Mountains, the Tujunga Wash, and Hansen Dam's park and water facilities. With Lancaster Lake and Pop's gone, as well as the swimming pools, the population felt a need for a recreational area of a great size. That work is proceeding. In 1971, it was estimated that from the outlying areas, there were 7.5 million people using the Angeles Forest streams and picnic areas.

There are still a few orange trees and grapevines to remind us of the past. There is no real industrial area, but there are now 16 schools, 9 formal churches, 58 service and social organizations, 3 websites, a hot line, and a public access television station. Population at last count is 43,000 with 16,000 households. The median income in 1989 was $42,000. The area still thrives on the beauty and spaciousness of the valley, canyons, and mountains. There is plenty of free space for horses and hikers. The area is now home to a diverse group of people from all walks of life.

To return to the beginning . . . what did those settlers who arrived in the 1880s to what is now Sunland-Tujunga have in them that would make it possible for them to make homes, a town, and a life on a frontier such as this one? Was it courage? Desperation? A certain eccentricity? How does a person arrive in a strange land with no home to go to, no markets or fast food restaurants, no phones, no electricity, and just a stream for running water? The stories told here are representative of the many Sunland-Tujunga citizens, throughout the area's growth, who have made enormous contributions for those of us who have come after their labors.

IMPROVEMENT ASSOCIATION. It was a struggle, but the Improvement Association was able to put markers on the two entrances to Sunland-Tujunga.

BIBLIOGRAPHY

Boesen, Victor. "California's 'Cure Town' for Asthmatics." *Coronet Magazine.* October 1952: p. 40.

Boule, Mary Null. *Mission San Fernando Rey de España*. Vashon: Merryant Publishing, 1988.

————. *Mission San Gabriel Archangel*. Vashon: Merryant Publishing, 1988.

Byar, Penny Terry. Personal interview by Marlene and Lloyd Hitt, November 15, 1999.

Conrad, Joan, and Donna Larson. *Docent Handbook of the Little Landers Historical Society*. Unpublished summary of local history, 1980 to present.

Franke, Lois Warren. *Memories of my Mother*. Unpublished memoir, March 2001.

Hall, Bolton. *A Little Land and a Living*. New York: Arcadia Press, 1908.

Irish, Ralph Seaton. *Ballads of Annexation or Songs That Went With Victory*. Self-published in Sunland, 1926.

Johnson, Lucille and Marion. "Two Women from the Canyon." Unpublished oral history recorded by Julia Stein.

Knight, Albert. *Stonehurst: A 1920s Era Stone House Neighborhood*. Self-published paper, April 2002.

Livingston, Alfred Jr. and Student Naturalists Association of the Audabon Society. *Geological Journeys in Southern California*. Dubuque: William C. Brown Company Publishers, 1933.

Lombard, Sarah. *Rancho Tujunga, A History of Sunland-Tujunga*. Burbank: The Bridge Publishing, 1990.

Los Angeles Corral of the Westerners. *Rancho Days in Southern California, Brand Book 20*. Studio City: Los Angeles Corral of the Westerners, 1997.

McCawley, William. *The First Angelinos, the Gabrielino Indians of Los Angeles*. Novato: Malki Museum Press/Ballena Press, 1952.

Morgan, Wallace and Mabel Hatch. "The Green Verdugo Hills, A Chronicle of Sunland-Tujunga, California and How it Grew." *Record Ledger, c.* 1953.

Pozzo, Mary Lou. *Hollywood Comes to Sunland-Tujunga 1920–1995*. Tujunga: Self-published booklet, 1995.

Record Ledger. Selected editions, 1923-1980.

Rowley, Robert. *Sunland-Tujunga*. Transcribed speech from the Bolton Hall Museum, *c.* 1985.

Robinson, John W. *The San Gabriels*: *Arcadia, California*. Big Santa Anita Historical Society, 1991.

Smythe, William Ellsworth. *City Homes on Country Lanes*. New York: Macmillan and Company, 1921.

Sunset Publishing Corporation. *The California Missions*. Menlo Park: Sunset Books, 1993.

Tiernan, Mary Lee. *Hotels for the Hopeful*. Sunland: Snoops Desktop Publishing, 1999.

Whelan, John and Bill Scott. "George Harris." Interview by Jack Wollard.

Glendale and Montrose Railway Company. www.erha.org/g&m.htm.

FLOOD DAMAGE. Floods often washed roads away.

INDEX

FLOOD CONTROL. Harry Zachau poses beside the check dams in Haines Canyon prior to the flood of 1938.